Grade **3**

Scott Foresman

On-Level
Take-Home Readers

ISBN: 0-328-20013-1
Copyright © Pearson Education, Inc.

9 10 V036 14 13 12

PEARSON
Scott
Foresman

Editorial Offices: Glenview, Illinois • Parsippany, New Jersey • New York, New York
Sales Offices: Boston, Massachusetts • Duluth, Georgia • Glenview, Illinois
Coppell, Texas • Sacramento, California • Mesa, Arizona

Contents

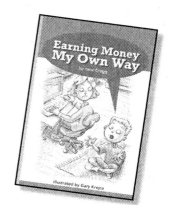

How to Use the Take-Home Leveled Readers

1. Tear out the pages for each Take-Home Leveled Reader. Make a copy for each student. Be sure to copy both sides of each page.

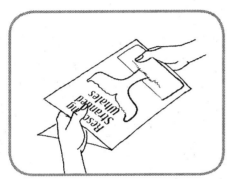

2. Fold the pages in half to make a booklet.

3. Staple the pages on the left-hand side.

4. Have students read and discuss the Take-Home Leveled Readers with family members.

Salt Lick
Boom Town

by Kristin Cashore

illustrated by David Sheldon

Suggested levels for Guided Reading, DRA,™
Lexile,® and Reading Recovery™ are provided
in the Pearson Scott Foresman Leveling Guide.

Genre	Comprehension Skills and Strategy
Animal fantasy	• Realism and Fantasy • Theme • Prior Knowledge

Scott Foresman Reading Street 3.1.1

ISBN 0-328-13323-X

9 780328 133239

90000

PEARSON

Scott
Foresman

Vocabulary

boom

coins

fetched

laundry

mending

pick

skillet

spell

Word count: 577

Note: The total word count includes words in the running text and headings only. Numerals and words in chapter titles, captions, labels, diagrams, charts, graphs, sidebars, and extra features are not included.

Reader Response

1. What things in this book tell you that it is a fantasy?

2. What do you know about boom towns? What makes the town in this book a boom town?

3. On a chart like the one below, write at least five past-tense words from this book that end in –*ed*. Then write the base words. Put a check next to the words in which you drop the final *e* before adding -*ed*.

Past-tense Word	Base Word

4. How could the animals in this book have made their community last longer? What could they have done differently?

Salt Lick
Boom Town

by Kristin Cashore

illustrated by David Sheldon

Editorial Offices: Glenview, Illinois • Parsippany, New Jersey • New York, New York
Sales Offices: Needham, Massachusetts • Duluth, Georgia • Glenview, Illinois
Coppell, Texas • Ontario, California • Mesa, Arizona

What Makes a Community?

A community is a group of people living and working in the same area. Every community needs certain things. For example, a community needs doctors. It needs schools for the children. It needs stores to buy food and clothing. It needs people who will make laws for the community.

Every person in a community is important. Teachers, lawyers, shopkeepers, waiters, writers, builders, artists, doctors, police officers—everyone plays an important role! Communities work well when people work well together.

ISBN: 0-328-13323-X

Copyright © Pearson Education, Inc.

All Rights Reserved. Printed in the United States of America. This publication is protected by Copyright, and permission should be obtained from the publisher prior to any prohibited reproduction, storage in a retrieval system, or transmission in any form by any means, electronic, mechanical, photocopying, recording, or likewise. For information regarding permission(s), write to: Permissions Department, Scott Foresman, 1900 East Lake Avenue, Glenview, Illinois 60025.

2 3 4 5 6 7 8 9 10 V0G1 14 13 12 11 10 09 08 07 06 05

Shelly was the only animal left. "Where did everyone go?" she asked. But no one was there to answer. "Well," she said, "I guess I'll start walking." And so she did.

15

Shelly the turtle liked to walk. She walked up hills. She walked over plains. She walked and walked all day. Shelly was a good walker.

One day, Shelly walked right into a salt lick. The salt was yummy on her tongue.

Shelly did something she had never done before. She stopped walking!

One by one, the animals left. Their families and their friends left. The cat that owned the bookstore left. The crocodile that ran the hot dog stand left.

Before long, the town was empty. The salt lick had become a ghost town.

The next day, Shelly was still at the salt lick. Before too long, Fuzzy the horse rode by on his bicycle. He stopped to see what Shelly was doing there.

"Yum," said Fuzzy. "Just wait until I tell my family about this salt lick."

"Well, I'll be," said Fuzzy. "I don't know about you, Pinky, but I think I'll move on. There must be another salt lick somewhere."

"I'll come with you," said Pinky.

"Me too," said the hippo.

"Me too," said the rabbit, the lizard, the raccoon, and the other animals. But Shelly the turtle did not say, "Me too."

The next day, Shelly, Fuzzy, and Fuzzy's family were still at the salt lick.

Pinky the pig rolled past on her roller skates, but then she stopped. She could tell that something big was going on.

"This salt sure is tasty!" said Pinky. "Just wait until I tell my friends."

Then one day, a strange thing happened. A hippo put her nose to the rock and licked. But it didn't taste like salt. It tasted like rock!

A rabbit sniffed the rock. No salt!

A lizard licked the rock. Nothing!

The salt was gone! The animals had licked it all away!

Soon Shelly, Fuzzy, Pinky, and all their friends and relatives were at the salt lick. But that was only the beginning.

Tales of the salt lick spread. Animals came from all corners of the globe. Zebras, moose, penguins, and bears came. All the animals wanted to be at the salt lick!

"This is the life," Fuzzy said.

All the animals agreed.

"Is the salt lick getting smaller?" Shelly asked.

"Do you think it's getting smaller?"

But no one heard her. They were too busy licking the salt.

A boom town grew around the salt lick. Animals spent their days there. They brought their newspapers to the salt lick. They brought their babies. Kittens chased string and puppies fetched sticks near the salt lick. Some animals brought their knitting and their mending. The animals also brought coins.

Before too long, the salt lick had hotels and restaurants. It had a gas station and a swimming pool. It had a museum full of paintings. There was even a roller coaster that ran right over the salt lick!

A clever raccoon built a store beside the salt lick. She sold ribbons and skillets and ladders and picks.

She also sold cold drinks. The salt made the animals thirsty. Business was good, especially during hot spells!

Soon the salt lick had a book store, a movie house, and a hot dog stand. Animals built houses near the salt lick. They built a place to do their laundry. They built a school and a park.

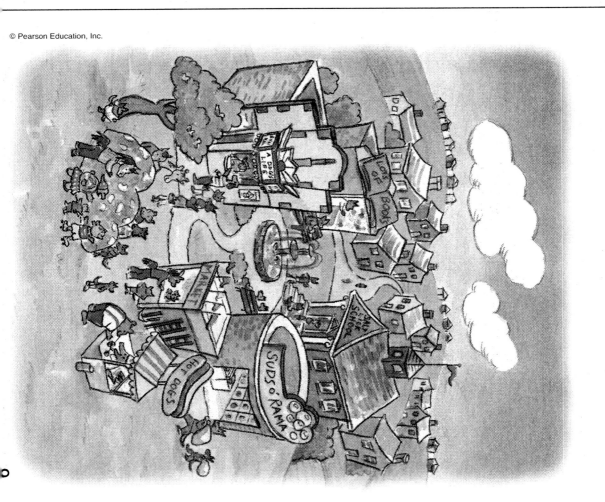

Social Studies

Let's Make a Trade!

by Marianne Lenihan

Genre	Comprehension Skills and Strategy	Text Features
Expository nonfiction	• Sequence • Draw Conclusions • Summarize	• Chart • Captions • Glossary

Scott Foresman Reading Street 3.1.2

ISBN 0-328-13326-4

9 780328 133260

90000

PEARSON

Scott
Foresman

Vocabulary

carpenter

carpetmaker

knowledge

marketplace

merchant

plenty

straying

thread

Word count: 450

Note: The total word count includes words in the running text and headings only. Numerals and words in chapter titles, captions, labels, diagrams, charts, graphs, sidebars, and extra features are not included.

Reader Response

1. Place these events of Bartering Day in order: some students bartered; students displayed their items; students brought items from home; students decided what to barter for.

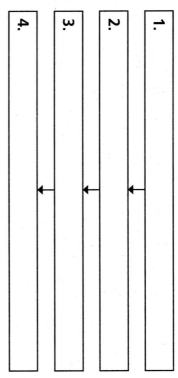

   1.

   2.

   3.

   4.

2. Summarize the bartering between the radio station and theater company.

3. *Straying* is used on page 6 as an adjective. Its base word can be a noun, an adjective, or a verb. Use the base word as a verb in a complete sentence.

4. What were the dads able to barter on pages 8 and 9?

Let's Make a Trade!

by Marianne Lenihan

Editorial Offices: Glenview, Illinois • Parsippany, New Jersey • New York, New York
Sales Offices: Needham, Massachusetts • Duluth, Georgia • Glenview, Illinois
Coppell, Texas • Ontario, California • Mesa, Arizona

Glossary

carpenter *n.* someone whose work is building and repairing things made of wood.

carpetmaker *n.* a person who makes carpets and rugs for floors.

knowledge *n.* what you know.

marketplace *n.* a place where people meet to buy and sell things.

merchant *n.* someone who buys and sells goods for a living.

plenty *n.* a full supply; all that you need; a large enough number or amount.

straying *adj.* wandering.

thread *n.* a very thin string made of strands of cotton, silk, wool, or nylon, spun and twisted together.

Every effort has been made to secure permission and provide appropriate credit for photographic material. The publisher deeply regrets any omission and pledges to correct errors called to its attention in subsequent editions.

Unless otherwise acknowledged, all photographs are the property of Scott Foresman, a division of Pearson Education.

Photo locators denoted as follows: Top (T), Center (C), Bottom (B), Left (L), Right (R), Background (Bkgd)

Opener: (TL) Getty Royalty Free, (TR) Getty Royalty Free, (BL) Rubberball, (BR) Rubberball; 1 Getty Royalty Free; 3 Rubberball; 4 ©DK Images; 5 ©DK Images; 6 Bridgeman; 7 ©DK Images; 8 Rubberball; 9 Rubberball; 10 ©DK Images; 11 ©DK Images; 14 Getty Royalty Free; 15 Corbis

ISBN: 0-328-13326-4

2 3 4 5 6 7 8 9 10 V0G1 14 13 12 11 10 09 08 07 06 05

Before you decide to barter anything, check with your parents! Your parents will know the value of almost everything in your house. They will know whether it's OK for you to barter something. Once you have permission, have fun bartering!

Talk to your parents first about the value of items you want to barter.

© Pearson Education, Inc.

Katie wants to learn to play the violin. Tina wants to learn to ride a bike. If they agree to teach one another these things, then Katie and Tina have bartered.

Bartering is trading goods, **knowledge,** or services with others. Barterers simply trade what they have for what they need.

Katie knows how to ride a bike.

Tina knows how to play the violin.

The next time you decide to trade an item or a chore, think about its value and the value of what you might be trading for. You might decide to wait for a better offer.

Bartering began thousands of years ago, before money was used. Farmers traded crops for cloth to make clothes. A blacksmith might have shoed the horse of a **merchant** in trade for an item from the merchant's store.

This merchant has beads to barter.

On Bartering Day, each student showed his or her item. The students then decided what they wanted to barter for.

Most students found items they wanted. Some made several trades before they were finished bartering. Others decided to keep their own items.

13

Two men barter goods in a medieval European marketplace.

Sometimes one person would have to trade several small things for one big thing to make the trade fair. Suppose a **carpenter** has a big table. A **carpetmaker** wants it. The carpetmaker might have to trade three or four small rugs for the big table.

To understand bartering better, a class of third graders decided to have a "Bartering Day" with their teacher's help. The students each brought one item to school that they no longer wanted.

Bartering Day!

Neighbors often joined together to trade. They built houses for new neighbors or barns for **straying** animals. Each neighbor knew that his or her work would be rewarded someday when he or she needed help.

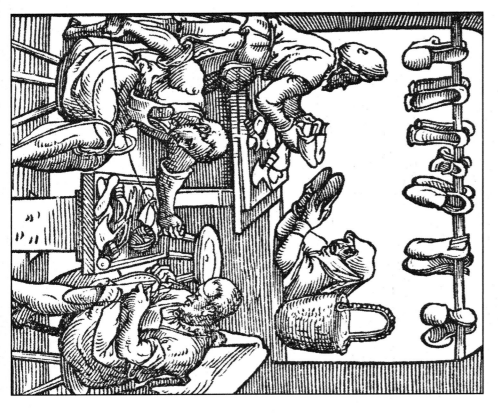

This woman is offering bread to trade for shoes.

Businesses barter with other businesses. What might bartering look like in the **marketplace**? Here is one example.

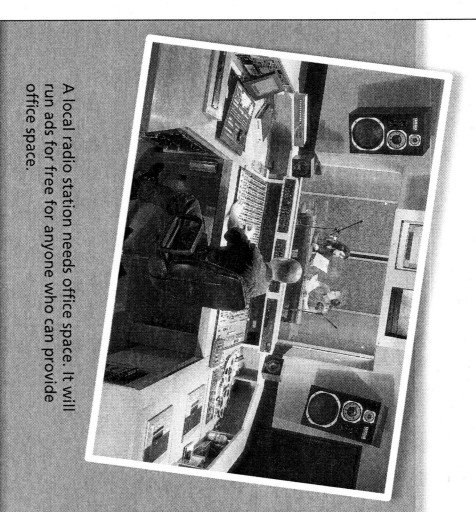

A local radio station needs office space. It will run ads for free for anyone who can provide office space.

SOLUTION: The community theater barters its office space for free advertising on the radio station.

American colonists and Native Americans traded for what they wanted and needed. Native Americans had **plenty** of furs to barter for the cloth, **thread**, and tools of the American colonists.

Today, people barter in many ways. Bartering partners can be found on the Internet and in newspapers and magazines. They can be found in your neighborhood.

A community theater company needs to advertise its summer plays, but it doesn't have enough money. It does have an entire floor of empty offices.

Bartering is also a way for a family to save money. Instead of using money to buy items or services, families may barter for what they need.

This way, they can keep their money in the bank and still get what they need. A family's bartering plan might look like this, once they have found another family to barter with them.

The Smith Family

Items or Services to Be Traded

Dad	Mom	Daughter	Daughter
knowledge of how to start a small business	bread machine	exercise equipment	collection of sports cards

The Jones Family

Items or Services to Be Traded

Dad	Mom	Daughter	Son
carpentry work	food processor	tutoring in math	bike and skateboard

Social Studies

Let's Save Money!

by Sharon Franklin
illustrated by Ruth Flanigan

Suggested levels for Guided Reading, DRA,™
Lexile,® and Reading Recovery™ are provided
in the Pearson Scott Foresman Leveling Guide.

Genre	Comprehension Skills and Strategy	Text Features
Narrative nonfiction	• Sequence • Author's Purpose • Visualize	• Charts • Glossary

Scott Foresman Reading Street 3.1.3

ISBN 0-328-13329-9

9 780328 133291

90000

PEARSON

Scott
Foresman

Vocabulary

college

dimes

downtown

fined

nickels

quarters

rich

Word count: 583

Note: The total word count includes words in the running text and headings only. Numerals and words in chapter titles, captions, labels, diagrams, charts, graphs, sidebars, and extra features are not included.

Reader Response

1. Reread page 12. Use a graphic organizer like this to explain Kyle's allowance and what he does with it.

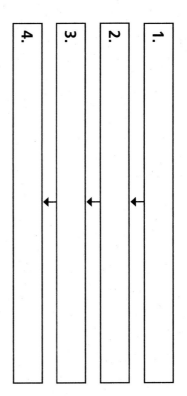

2. What did you see in your mind as you read page 8?

3. What do the words *nickels*, *dimes*, and *quarters* have in common? Use the three words in three complete sentences.

4. Find the graphs on page 7. How much money was there after five years? After ten years?

Let's Save Money!

by Sharon Franklin

illustrated by Ruth Flanigan

PEARSON

Scott Foresman

Editorial Offices: Glenview, Illinois • Parsippany, New Jersey • New York, New York
Sales Offices: Needham, Massachusetts • Duluth, Georgia • Glenview, Illinois
Coppell, Texas • Ontario, California • Mesa, Arizona

Glossary

college *n.* a school of higher learning, where a person can study after high school, that gives degrees or diplomas.

dimes *n.* coins of the United States and Canada equal to ten cents.

downtown *n.* The main part or business part of a town or city.

fined *v.* made to pay money as punishment for breaking a law or regulation.

nickels *n.* coins of the United States and Canada equal to five cents.

quarters *n.* coins of the United States and Canada equal to twenty-five cents.

rich *adj.* having a great deal of money, land, goods, or other property.

16

Every effort has been made to secure permission and provide appropriate credit for photographic material. The publisher deeply regrets any omission and pledges to correct errors called to its attention in subsequent editions.

Unless otherwise acknowledged, all photographs are the property of Scott Foresman, a division of Pearson Education.

Photo locators denoted as follows: Top (T), Center (C), Bottom (B), Left (L), Right (R), Background (Bkgd)

Illustrations by Ruth Flanigan

ISBN: 0-328-13329-9

Once you have your plan worked out, you can make it work. Keep your goal in mind and don't give up. You'll have fun watching your money grow!

Megan was a saver. She saved every letter her grandmother sent her. She always saved the pointy end of her ice cream cone for last. She had even saved a kitten from drowning!

But Megan's friend Kyle had saved more money than she had. Megan was puzzled about how he did it.

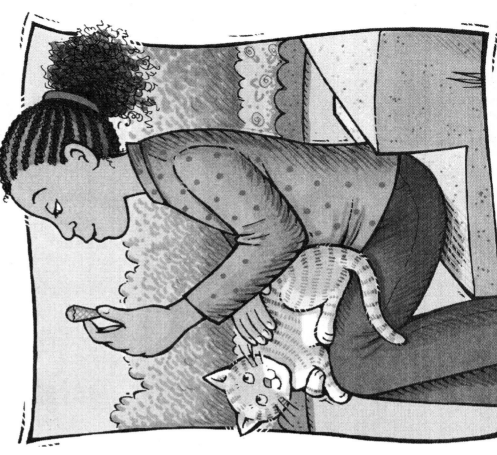

Ask an adult to help you get started on a savings plan. Remember to make a plan that allows you to save money but gives you some spending money too.

Megan and Kyle had each saved $10.00 a month for one year. At the end of the year, they compared their money. Megan had $120.00 and Kyle had more. Megan didn't understand why. She asked her mom to help solve the puzzle.

As you can see, it is possible to save your money and still have some left over to spend. **Nickels**, **dimes**, and **quarters** quickly add up to dollars. And with interest earned in a bank savings account, you may be **rich** in savings sooner than you think!

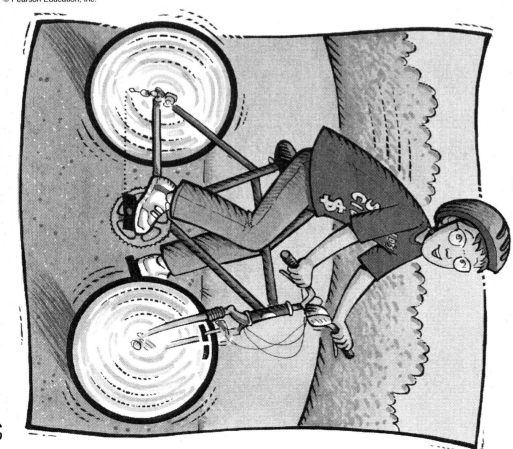

Mom explained that Megan and Kyle had saved their money in two different ways. Megan had saved her money in her piggy bank. But Kyle had saved his money in a bank savings account. Mom said that money grows in a bank savings account. Let's find out how money can grow.

Kyle receives an allowance of five dollars a week. Each week he puts two dollars into his savings account. Kyle donates one dollar to a food bank at the grocery store for people who do not have enough to eat. Finally, Kyle keeps two dollars to spend for himself!

Banks earn money by lending out the money you deposit, or put into your bank account. Since the bank uses your money, it pays you interest. Your money will earn interest for as long as you keep it in the bank. If you need to take money out of your bank account, you will not be **fined**.

Then the teller told Megan about the bank savings club. Members received a prize after every ten deposits. Megan was excited to be a savings club member!

11

Imagine putting $5,000.00 in a savings account for **college**. The bank pays 5 percent yearly interest. After a year, there would be $5,250.00 in the account. The extra $250.00 is the interest earned. In five years the account would grow to $6,381.41. And in ten years, there would be $8,144.47 in your college account!

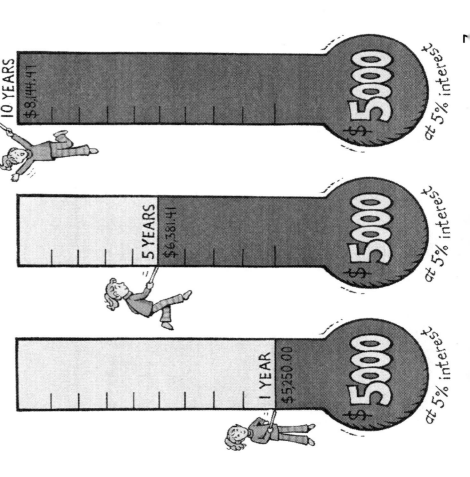

10 YEARS
$8,144.47

5 YEARS
$6,381.41

1 YEAR
$5,250.00

$5000 at 5% interest

$5000 at 5% interest

$5000 at 5% interest

At the bank, Megan wrote her name, address, and other information on a form. She gave the bank teller her first five-dollar deposit. The teller gave Megan a book to record her deposits. She showed Megan the kind of statement she would receive four times each year. The statement would show her deposits and interest.

DATE MEMO INTEREST WITHDRAWALS DEPOSITS BALANCE

DATE DESCRIPTION OF TRANSACTION AMOUNT OF WITHDRAWAL AMOUNT OF DEPOSIT OR INTEREST BALANCE

Before you open a savings account, ask yourself four questions: *Why do I want to save money? How much do I want to save? When will I need the money? How much can I save each week or month?*

In January Megan decided she'd like to save one hundred dollars for a family trip that June. If she saved five dollars each week, she would reach her goal. This time, Megan wanted to save her money at a bank. Megan and her mom went **downtown** to open a savings account!

Earning Money My Own Way

by Jane Cregg

Suggested levels for Guided Reading, DRA,
Lexile,® and Reading Recovery™ are provided
in the Pearson Scott Foresman Leveling Guide.

Genre	Comprehension Skills and Strategy
Realistic fiction	• Realism and Fantasy • Character • Monitor and Fix Up

Scott Foresman Reading Street 3.1.4

PEARSON

Scott Foresman

ISBN 0-328-13332-9

9 780328 133321

90000

Vocabulary

amount

check

earn

expensive

interest

million

thousand

value

worth

Word count: 625

Note: The total word count includes words in the running text and headings only. Numerals and words in chapter titles, captions, labels, diagrams, charts, graphs, sidebars, and extra features are not included.

Reader Response

1. Could this story really happen? Why or why not?

2. Reread pages 4 and 5. Tell the order of Andy's ideas when he thought about ways to get money for the concert ticket. Use a chart like the one below to help organize your thoughts.

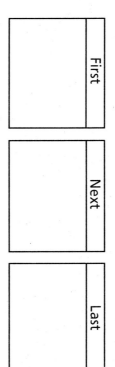

First	Next	Last

3. *Interest* appears with different meanings on pages 8 and 13. Use a dictionary to tell which definition is used on each page.

4. If you were in Andy's situation, how would you have earned the money? Explain why.

Earning Money My Own Way

by Jane Cregg

illustrated by Gary Krejca

Editorial Offices: Glenview, Illinois • Parsippany, New Jersey • New York, New York
Sales Offices: Needham, Massachusetts • Duluth, Georgia • Glenview, Illinois
Coppell, Texas • Ontario, California • Mesa, Arizona

Saving Energy Equals Saving Money!

Did you know there are many things you can do at home that will help save money? Here are two examples:

Electricity and water cost money. Each month, your parents pay for the electricity and water you use. The less you waste those two resources, the more you'll help your family save money!

It's very easy to save electricity. Just make sure to turn off the lights whenever you leave a room. As for water, check the faucets to see if they're dripping. If they are, then tighten them! By taking such simple steps, you can help your whole family save money.

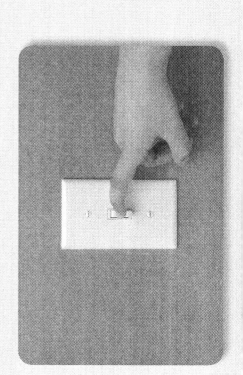

16

ISBN: 0-328-13332-9

Copyright © Pearson Education, Inc.

All Rights Reserved. Printed in the United States of America. This publication is protected by Copyright, and permission should be obtained from the publisher prior to any prohibited reproduction, storage in a retrieval system, or transmission in any form by any means, electronic, mechanical, photocopying, recording, or likewise. For information regarding permission(s), write to: Permissions Department, Scott Foresman, 1900 East Lake Avenue, Glenview, Illinois 60025.

2 3 4 5 6 7 8 9 10 V0G1 14 13 12 11 10 09 08 07 06 05

"Andy, you did a wonderful job!" Mr. Thornton exclaimed. "Here's a check for the money you earned. Are you planning to do anything special with it?" Mr. Thornton asked curiously.

"Very special!" Andy said, thrilled. "I'm going to see my favorite band in concert!"

"That sounds exciting," Mr. Thornton replied. "Have a great time!"

15

At last, the summer had arrived! Andy was on vacation from school until September. There was going to be a concert in town in July, and his favorite band was playing. Andy didn't want to miss the chance to see them perform.

Andy spent ten days working in Mr. Thornton's yard. He pulled weeds in the garden. He mowed and watered the lawn. Andy also remembered to collect the mail, just as Mr. Thornton had asked.

Mr. Thornton arrived home on June 30. He called Andy on the telephone, and Andy hurried next door to collect his money.

Andy's parents agreed to take him to the concert if he saved half the money for his ticket. *How can I save the money I need?* Andy wondered.

Then he thought of three ways to get it. He could work for it. He could borrow it. Or, if he were lucky, he might be given some money as a gift!

"Fifteen dollars sounds just fine," Mr. Thornton replied. "That's a good value for your hard work. And don't worry. You'll get paid on time. I don't like to pay interest! I'll be on vacation from June 20 through June 29. So those are the days you'll need to work."

Andy couldn't think of anyone who might loan him the money. Then he thought about gifts. *That won't work*, he thought. *My birthday is four months away.* Finally, Andy tried to think of ways he could work for the money. He decided to ask his big sister, Liz, for advice.

"Well, how about a thousand dollars?" Andy joked. "Oh, don't worry, Mr. Thornton. I'm only kidding!" Andy said. "I would never make it that expensive. Does fifteen dollars sound OK?"

Andy knocked on Liz's bedroom door. "Hi, Sis," he said. "I'm asking Mom and Dad to take me to the concert next month. But the ticket prices are sky high! Do you have any ideas how I can earn money to pay for my share of the ticket?"

"Why, yes!" said Mr. Thornton. "I was just sitting here thinking that I should ask for help. Will you do it, Andy? I'll pay you to work in my yard. I'll also pay you to collect my mail," he added. Then he asked, "What amount shall I pay you?"

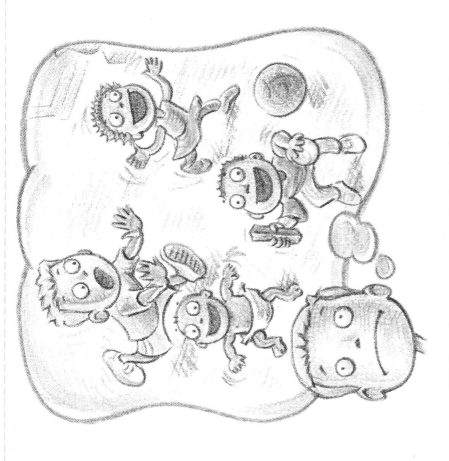

"Why don't you try babysitting with me?" Liz replied. "That's what I do."

Andy had helpd Liz watch their cousins a few weeks earlier. He hadn't enjoyed babysitting at all!

"But Liz, I can't stand babysitting," Andy complained.

Andy knew that Mr. Thornton would be going on vacation soon. He walked over to Mr. Thornton's house to ask him if he needed more help with the garden.

"Hi," Andy said, spotting Mr. Thornton on his porch. "I was wondering if you need someone to care for your garden while you're away."

"Then try to think of an interest you have and start there," Liz suggested.

"OK," Andy said as he left his sister's room to think.

Andy thought about what he really liked to do. Earlier that week he had helped weed his neighbor's garden. It had been fun!

Mr. Thornton was getting older, and he needed a helper to pull weeds. He had offered to pay Andy, but Andy said he'd work for free. When Andy had finished his work, Mr. Thornton had said, "It's worth a million dollars to see my garden without those weeds!"

ONE CHILI PEPPER

~ by Kristin Cashore ~

Genre	Comprehension Skills and Strategy
Realistic fiction	• Character and Setting • Generalize • Story Structure

Scott Foresman Reading Street 3.1.5

ISBN 0-328-13335-3

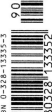

9 780328 133352

90000

PEARSON

Scott
Foresman

Vocabulary

arranged

bundles

dangerously

errands

excitedly

steady

unwrapped

wobbled

Word count: 722

Reader Response

1. What is the main setting of this story?

2. Use a chart like the one below to put these events from the story in order: Amelia bought a chili pepper; Pots and pans wobbled on a stand; A man bought a sombrero.

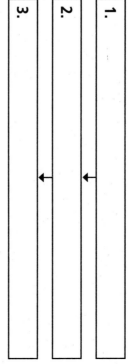

1. _____

2. _____

3. _____

3. On a sheet of paper, write at least three words from this story that end in –ing. Write the base word for each. Then write each word in a complete sentence.

4. Amelia is learning about Mexican culture. Is there a place you would like to go to study a culture? Why?

ONE CHILI PEPPER

~ by Kristin Cashore ~
illustrated by Janet Nelson

PEARSON

Scott
Foresman

Editorial Offices: Glenview, Illinois • Parsippany, New Jersey • New York, New York
Sales Offices: Parsippany, New Jersey • Duluth, Georgia • Glenview, Illinois
Coppell, Texas • Ontario, California • Mesa, Arizona

The Tianguis

In many neighborhoods in Mexico, there is an open-air market held in the street once a week. This market is called a *tianguis*. Traveling vendors set up stands in the street and sell their wares. Pots, pans, toys, shoes, meat, vegetables—many things can be found at the tianguis!

A tianguis is full of colorful sights and wonderful smells. It is a Mexican tradition. It is also a good way to buy the week's groceries at a good price.

At the end of the day, the sellers take down their stands and pack up their wares. The street is quiet again—until the next week!

16

Every effort has been made to secure permission and provide appropriate credit for photographic material. The publisher deeply regrets any omission and pledges to correct errors called to its attention in subsequent editions.

Unless otherwise acknowledged, all photographs are the property of Scott Foresman, a division of Pearson Education.

Photo locators denoted as follows: Top (T), Center (C), Bottom (B), Left (L), Right (R), Background (Bkgd)

Illustrations by Janet Nelson

Photograph 16 Getty Images

ISBN: 0-328-13335-3

2 3 4 5 6 7 8 9 10 V0G1 14 13 12 11 10 09 08 07 06 05

Ben and Amelia started home with the chili pepper. Amelia smiled at all the pretty colors and the cheerful people.

When they reached their building, Amelia took one last look at the market. "Our shopping has been a great success," she said.

"It sure has!" Ben said.

Then Ben and Amelia went inside to tell Dad about their adventure.

15

"Oh, rats!" Dad said.

Amelia looked into the kitchen. Dad was standing at the counter with Amelia's brother, Ben. They were chopping vegetables.

"What's wrong, Dad?" Amelia asked.

"We forgot to get a chili pepper," Dad said.

"I could run down to the store for one," Amelia said.

Amelia opened her mouth to argue. But then she remembered. The smallest coin in Mexico is ten centavos! Nothing could cost less than that!

"That is a very good price," she said.

"But of course!" said the man.

Amelia gave the man a ten centavos coin. Ben chose a shiny red chili pepper. "*Muchas gracias*!" Ben and Amelia said. "Thank you very much."

Amelia and her family had been living in Mexico for only a week. Amelia's mother was going to teach at a school there for a year. Amelia and her family lived on the third floor of their building. The supermarket was just down the street. Amelia knew a little Spanish—enough to buy a chili pepper.

Finally they came to a stand piled high with many kinds of peppers. A big, smiling man stood behind a mountain of chili peppers. Amelia was ready to bargain.

"I need one chili pepper," she said in Spanish.

"Only one chili pepper?" asked the man. "That will be ten centavos, please."

"That would be great, Amelia!" Dad said.

"Ben, will you go with her?"

"Sure!" said Ben.

Dad gave Amelia some change. Amelia ran down the stairs, and Ben followed. Amelia burst onto the street.

Then she rubbed her eyes. She put her hand against the building to steady herself. She couldn't believe what she was seeing!

Amelia and Ben kept walking. There were so many sights and sounds. Everyone was talking.

"Everything smells so good!" Amelia said.

"I have never seen so many fruits and vegetables in my life!" Ben said.

Amelia's street was usually peaceful and calm. There weren't many people who lived there. It was a very quiet neighborhood.

But the street had changed! There were hundreds of people walking around. There were big stands made of wood and metal. People were selling all sorts of things at the stands. Her quiet street was noisy and colorful!

Ben stepped into the street behind Amelia. "Wow!" he said. "What's going on?"

"No," said the hat seller. "That is not enough." Then the hat seller told the man a new price. Finally, they agreed. The man paid for the hat and left. He seemed very happy.

"Wow," said Amelia. "I guess at this market you're supposed to bargain for a lower price."

6

11

Ben and Amelia stood at the edge of the crowd. At a stand nearby, a man arranged pots and pans on a table. He stacked them on top of each other. They wobbled dangerously, but they did not fall.

At another stand, a woman unwrapped bundles of brightly colored cloth. She shook them out so that everyone could see them. Amelia's eyes took in the colors of pink, yellow, green, and orange.

Amelia and Ben stopped at a hat stand. A man was buying a big straw hat with a wide brim called a *sombrero*. The hat seller told the man a price.

"No," said the man. "That is too much." The man offered the hat seller a lower price.

The stands stretched all the way down the street. Amelia could see toys, lamps, shoes, fish, meat, fruits, and vegetables. People walked up and down the street, doing their errands.

"It's an open-air market," Ben said.

"Hey, Ben," Amelia said, "do you think we could buy Dad's chili pepper at this market?"

"I don't see why not," Ben said.

Amelia and Ben stepped into the crowd. They walked past a stand with flowers. They saw a stand with watermelons.

One man stood behind a big pile of carrots and onions. He called out excitedly in Spanish, and Amelia understood him.

"Buy my carrots and onions! I have the best carrots and onions!" he shouted.

Suggested levels for Guided Reading, DRA,
Lexile,® and Reading Recovery™ are provided
in the Pearson Scott Foresman Leveling Guide.

Science

Genre	Comprehension Skills and Strategy	Text Features
Expository nonfiction	• Main Idea and Details • Compare and Contrast • Graphic Organizers	• Labels • Map • Glossary

Scott Foresman Reading Street 3.2.1

PEARSON
Scott Foresman

ISBN 0-328-13338-8
9 780328 133383 90000

Science

Life Science

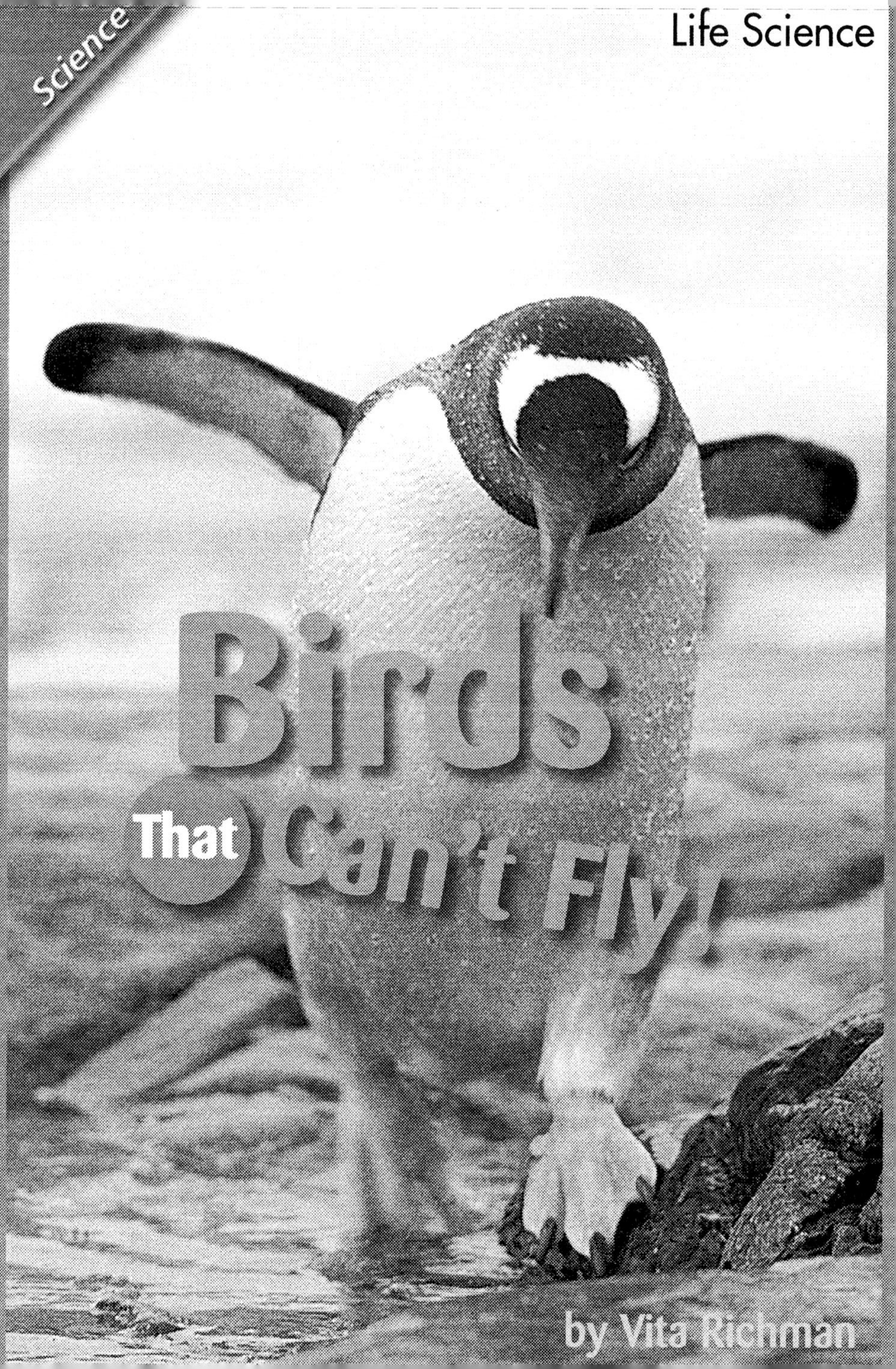

Birds That Can't Fly!

by Vita Richman

Vocabulary

cuddles

flippers

frozen

hatch

pecks

preen

snuggles

Word count: 651

Note: The total word count includes words in the running text and headings only. Numerals and words in chapter titles, captions, labels, diagrams, charts, graphs, sidebars, and extra features are not included.

Reader Response

1. What is the main idea of this selection?

2. Use a chart like the one below to put the cassowary, male ostrich, and flightless cormorant in order by weight.

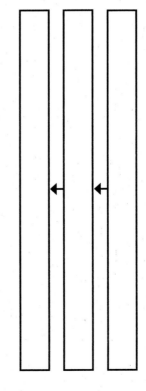

3. Write one sentence that uses *hatch* as a noun and another sentence that uses *hatch* as a verb. You may need to use a dictionary.

4. The map on pages 8 and 9 shows flightless birds living in or on many different countries, continents, and islands. Which of the flightless birds lives closest to the United States?

Glossary

cuddle *v.* to lie closely and comfortably; curl up.

flippers *n.* broad, flat body parts used for swimming by animals such as seals and penguins.

frozen *adj.* hardened with cold; turned into ice.

hatch *v.* to bring forth young; open.

pecks *v.* strikes at with the beak.

preen *v.* to smooth or arrange the feathers with the beak.

snuggle *v.* to lie closely and comfortably together; nestle; cuddle.

Birds That Can't Fly!

by Vita Richman

PEARSON
Scott Foresman

Editorial Offices: Glenview, Illinois • Parsippany, New Jersey • New York, New York
Sales Offices: Needham, Massachusetts • Duluth, Georgia • Glenview, Illinois
Coppell, Texas • Ontario, California • Mesa, Arizona

Wow! We have taken quite a tour of the world of flightless birds! From emus to kiwis to ostriches, you have now learned much about these unique creatures. Here are a few more interesting facts about flightless birds.

Flightless-Bird Facts

Ostrich fossils date back five million years.

There may be as many as 725,000 emus living today.

Kakapos are in danger of becoming extinct.

Cassowaries can live for more than sixty years.

15

Many birds cannot fly! They are called flightless birds.

Flightless birds are different from flying birds. Their bones are heavier than those of flying birds. Flightless birds' feathers are different too.

Like humans, all birds have a sternum, or breastbone. A flightless bird's sternum is different from that of a flying bird since there are no flight muscles attached to it.

Owl's skeleton

Penguin's skeleton

Have you ever eaten a kiwi fruit? There is a flightless bird called the kiwi. It lives in New Zealand. A kiwi is about the size of a chicken.

Kiwis have very long beaks with nostrils at the end. Their nostrils help them smell the insects and worms they like to eat. The kiwis' whiskers help them feel their way through tight spaces.

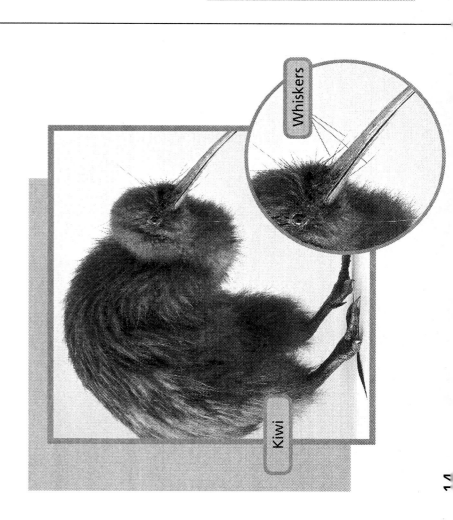

Whiskers

Kiwi

Penguins are flightless birds that swim underwater. They have **flippers** instead of wings. Many penguins live on and around the **frozen** continent of Antarctica.

You may have seen penguins in an aquarium **cuddle** and **snuggle** with their chicks. Have you ever watched a penguin **preen**, or clean and smooth its feathers?

Penguin

Kagus live on the island of New Caledonia in the South Pacific Ocean. They are called "the ghosts of the forest" because of their pale gray feathers. They like to eat snails, worms, and lizards.

Kagus are endangered because of hunting by dogs and cats. And kagu parents raise only one chick a year.

Kagu

13

Ostriches are the largest birds in the world. They live in Africa. Male ostriches can weigh three hundred pounds!

Ostriches eat plants. Female ostriches lay up to twelve eggs over a period of about three weeks. Both parents guard the nest while waiting for the eggs to **hatch.** An egg hatches when the chick inside **pecks** its way out of it.

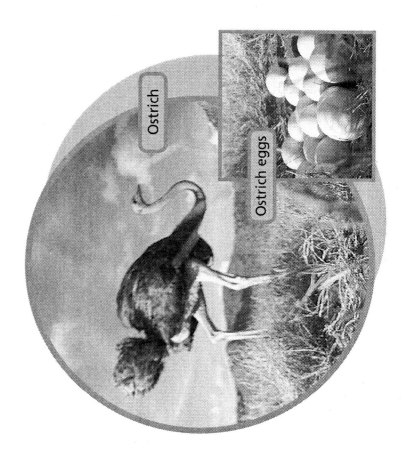

Ostrich

Ostrich eggs

Kakapos are parrots found in New Zealand. They have shiny, yellow-green feathers. The feathers on their faces make them look like owls.

Kakapos live alone. When it is time to mate, male kakapos make a booming sound to attract females. The sound of male kakapos booming can be heard from more than four miles away.

Kakapo

6

Emus live in Australia. They have shaggy, gray-brown feathers and long, powerful legs.

Emus eat fruit, seeds, plants, and insects. Female emus can lay up to ten bluish-green eggs at one time. Male emus sit on the nests for about fifty-five days, until the chicks hatch.

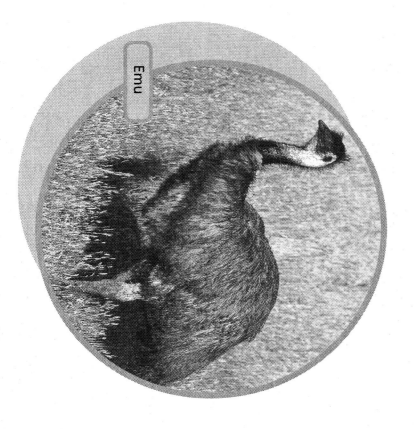

Emu

Flightless cormorants are rare. They are found only on the Galápagos Islands. They have few feathers and are black in color. They weigh about nine pounds.

Flightless cormorants have webbed feet and are great swimmers. When flightless cormorants come back to shore after a swim, they hold out their wings to dry.

Flightless cormorant

11

Cassowaries are found in the swamps and rain forests of Australia and New Guinea. They have crests on their heads. They have sharp claws and three toes on each foot.

Cassowaries weigh about 130 pounds. They eat fruit, insects, frogs, and snakes.

Cassowary

The common rhea lives in Brazil and Argentina. It has large eyes and a long neck. Rheas have three toes on each foot. When they run, they use their wings to change direction quickly.

Several female rheas lay up to eighty eggs in one nest. A male rhea cares for the chicks in the nest. He guards the chicks so well that he chases the female rheas away!

Rhea

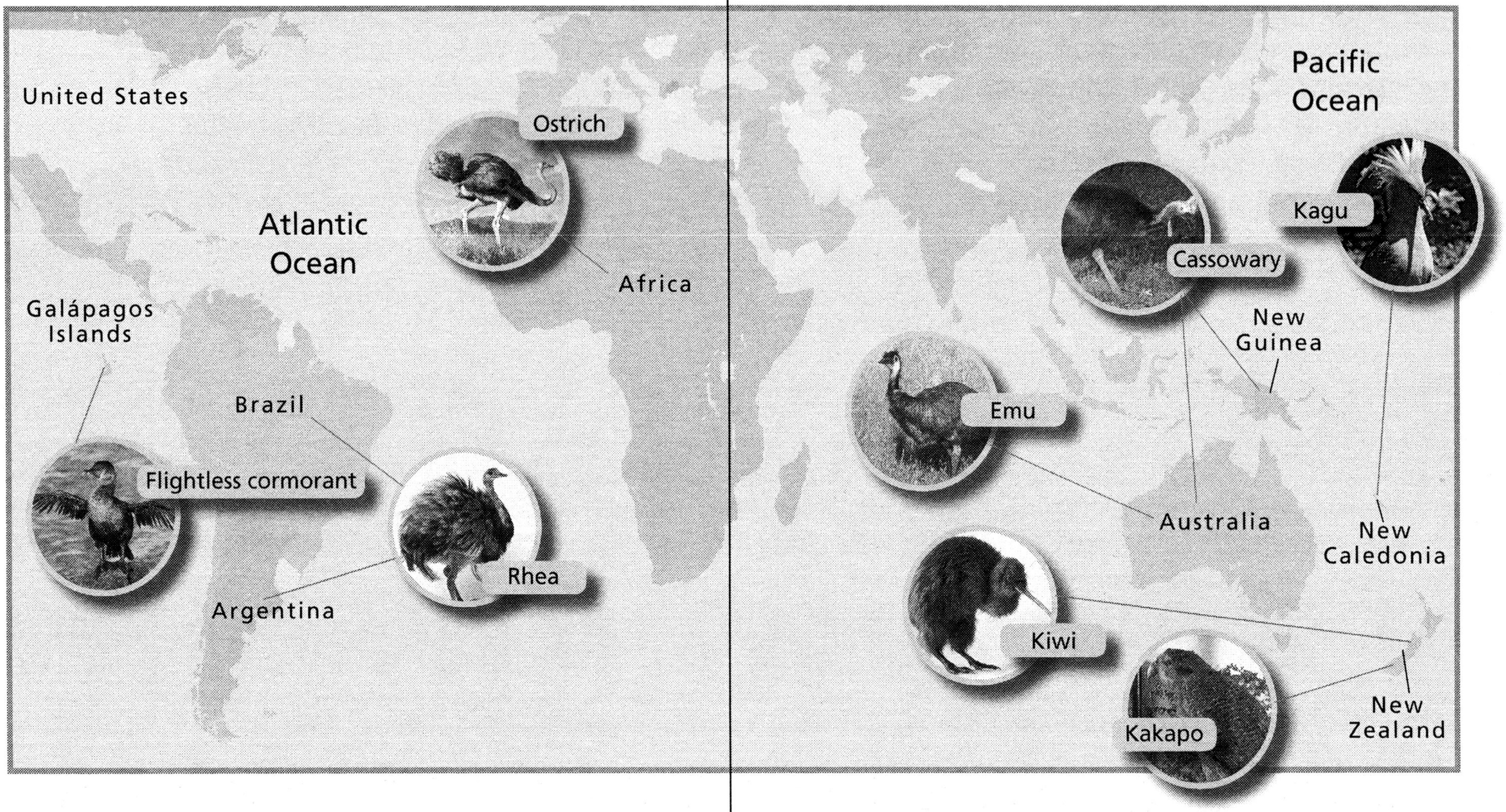

Galápagos
Islands

Flightless cormorant

Argentina

Brazil

Atlantic
Ocean

Rhea

Ostrich

Africa

This world map shows the homes of
many flightless birds. Do any of these
birds live in the country where you live?
Have you ever traveled to a country where
flightless birds live?

Emu

Kiwi

Kakapo

Australia

Cassowary

New
Guinea

New
Caledonia

Kagu

Pacific
Ocean

New
Zealand

Scientists believe that the ancestors
of flightless birds could fly. Scientists also
think that flightless birds became flightless
because the animals that once hunted
them became extinct.

Katy's Last-Minute Book Report

by Sasha Griffin

Suggested levels for Guided Reading, DRA,™
Lexile,® and Reading Recovery™ are provided
in the Pearson Scott Foresman Leveling Guide.

Genre	Comprehension Skills and Strategy	
Realistic fiction	• Main Idea • Sequence • Monitor and Fix Up	

Scott Foresman Reading Street 3.2.3

PEARSON

Scott Foresman

ISBN 0-328-13344-2

9 780328 133444

90000

Vocabulary

collection

enormous

realize

scattered

shiny

strain

Word count: 831

Note: The total word count includes words in the running text and headings only.
Numerals and words in chapter titles, captions, labels, diagrams, charts, graphs, sidebars, and extra features are not included.

Reader Response

1. What was the main idea of the story?

2. On a web like the one below, write *Katy missed . . .* in the middle oval. Then write the four activities that Katy missed out on because she hadn't completed her book report.

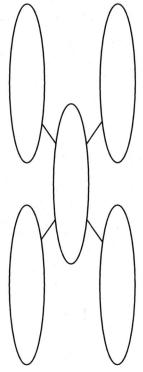

3. Find the base words of *information* and *collection*. Write two sentences using each base word.

4. If you found yourself in a situation like Katy's, what would you do?

Katy's Last-Minute Book Report

by Sasha Griffin
illustrated by Tom LaBaff

PEARSON
Scott
Foresman

Editorial Offices: Glenview, Illinois • Parsippany, New Jersey • New York, New York
Sales Offices: Needham, Massachusetts • Duluth, Georgia • Glenview, Illinois
Coppell, Texas • Ontario, California • Mesa, Arizona

Planning Your Time

Third-grade students have many things to do each day. Homework, sports, and family activities take up a lot of time. It can be hard to decide *what* to do *when*.

Can you think of some ideas for planning your time well? Here's a list that one student started. Add your own ideas to the list.

1. Make a calendar for the week.
2. Write things to do for the week on the calendar.
3.
4.
5.

Every effort has been made to secure permission and provide appropriate credit for photographic material. The publisher deeply regrets any omission and pledges to correct errors called to its attention in subsequent editions.

Unless otherwise acknowledged, all photographs are the property of Scott Foresman, a division of Pearson Education.

Photo locators denoted as follows: Top (T), Center (C), Bottom (B), Left (L), Right (R), Background (Bkgd)

Illustrations by Tom LaBaff

ISBN: 0-328-13344-2

During book share on Monday, Katy explained some interesting facts about horses. She answered a few questions too.

At the end of the day, Mr. Hayes reminded his students, "Your descriptive paragraphs are due on Friday."

As Katy and Pam walked home, Katy said, "Let's go to my house and work on our paragraphs. I'm not leaving anything until the last minute ever again!"

It was Monday afternoon and almost time to go home. Mr. Hayes pointed to the assignment on the board.

Katy read, "Book Reports due Monday." "Our monthly book share will be next Monday," Mr. Hayes reminded them. "Sharing your interesting reports and colorful posters is a great way for us to learn about books that are new to us. Your reports will encourage us to read those books!"

Katy began writing her book report on Sunday morning, and by lunchtime she had finished.

That afternoon Katy looked for poster paper, but she had none. She taped two pieces of lined paper together and drew with her crummy old crayons.

"This looks awful," Katy complained to her mom. "I don't want to turn it in."

"I think this project has taught you an important lesson," her mom said.

Katy walked home with her friend Pam. "What book are you going to write about?" Pam asked.

"I don't know," said Katy.

"Haven't you started yet?" Pam looked surprised. "I'm already finished reading mine."

"We still have a whole week," Katy said. "There's plenty of time."

Katy finally finished her book Saturday night. She thought about everything she would have to do the next day to finish her report on time. She had the report to write, and she also had the poster to do.

"I don't even know if I have poster paper," Katy worried. "Why did I wait until the last minute to do this?"

At that moment, the girls were in front of the library. "There's the library," said Pam. "Maybe you should look for a book."

"That's a good idea," replied Katy.

Inside the library Katy found a book about horses.

"That looks good," said Pam.

"I think it does too," Katy agreed. "I'm going to check it out. I will start reading it tonight right after soccer practice."

Katy read for the rest of Saturday. She had just started the last chapter when the phone rang. It was Pam.

"We're going out for pizza and a movie," Pam said. "Can you come?"

"I can't," Katy groaned. "I still have to work on my book report. I wish I'd started it earlier, like you!"

But Katy was too tired to read after soccer practice. "I'll start the book tomorrow," she told herself firmly.

Tuesday came, and Katy watched TV for a few hours after school. Then, after dinner, she worked on her coin collection until bedtime. She loved her shiny coins.

"It's too late to read now," Katy decided. "Tomorrow I'll start it for sure."

Katy did not enjoy the game. She was worried about finishing her book. She even tried reading during halftime, but it was hard to concentrate.

"Who wants to go out for ice cream?" asked the coach after the game.

"We do!" shouted everyone but Katy.

"I wish I could," Katy said. "But I have a book report to do."

"That's too bad!" said the coach. "We'll miss you!"

"Do you want to come over?" Katy asked Pam after school on Wednesday. They were both walking home.

Pam shook her head. "I have to work on my book report. Are you liking your horse book?"

"I'm going to start it today," Katy said.

"Boy! You always leave things until the last minute!" Pam exclaimed.

"It's not the last minute," Katy told her. "I still have four whole days left."

Katy ate breakfast Saturday morning. Then she went right back to her room to read her horse book.

"At least I have the whole weekend," she thought.

There was a knock on her door. "Do you realize you have a soccer game in half an hour?" asked Dad.

"Oh, no!" wailed Katy. She quickly put on her uniform and grabbed her book. "I'll have to read in the car."

When Katy arrived home, her mom was waiting for her. "Your room is an enormous mess!" she scolded. "Things are scattered everywhere! Please clean it up!"

"But I have to read my book," Katy answered.

"Your room comes first," Mom said. It took Katy hours to put her stuff away. By the time she was done, she was too tired to read. So Katy put off starting her book until Thursday.

Katy finally began reading her book on Thursday. It wasn't easy. The book had so much new information that Katy had to strain to understand it. By bedtime she had read only a few pages.

On Friday night Katy's brother asked, "Aren't you going to watch a video with us? It's your turn to choose."

"I can't," said Katy. "I have to read."

Our Garden

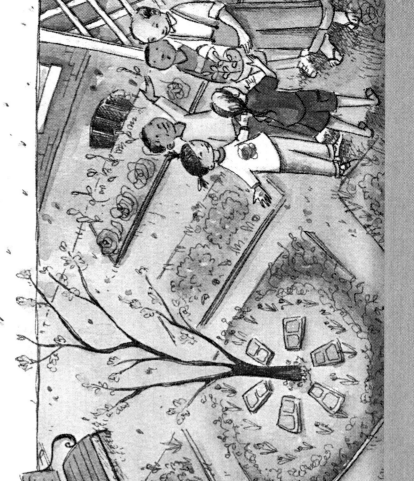

by Jessica Quilty

illustrated by Nicole Wong

Genre	Comprehension Skills and Strategy
Realistic fiction	• Author's Purpose • Plot • Predict

Scott Foresman Reading Street 3.2.4

PEARSON

Scott
Foresman

ISBN 0-328-13347-7

9 780328 133475

90000

Vocabulary

bottom
cheat
clever
crops
lazy
partners
wealth

Word count: 1,032

Reader Response

1. What was the author's purpose in describing what the lot had looked like before the kids started working on it?

2. Now that the garden has been opened up to the people of the city, what do you predict will happen to it?

3. The word *crops* is used as a noun in this story. It can also be used as a verb. Find out what the word *crops* means when it is a verb. Write the word *crops* in a complete sentence using that meaning.

4. If you were Mayor Smith, which rules for using the garden would you make for the people of the city? Write four rules on a web like the one below.

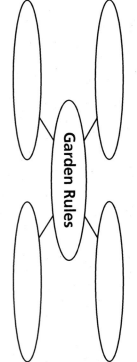

Garden Rules

Our Garden

by Jessica Quilty

illustrated by Nicole Wong

PEARSON

Scott Foresman

Editorial Offices: Glenview, Illinois • Parsippany, New Jersey • New York, New York
Sales Offices: Needham, Massachusetts • Duluth, Georgia • Glenview, Illinois
Coppell, Texas • Ontario, California • Mesa, Arizona

Kids Help Out!

There are many ways you can help out your community and your neighbors. Turning an old lot into a garden may be just the beginning!

The Youth Volunteer Corps is an organization with branches all over the United States. In the Youth Volunteer Corps, kids help out every day by spending time with elderly or disabled people, tutoring other children, cleaning up parks and beaches, serving meals to the needy, and much more. Find out what you can do today to help out in your community!

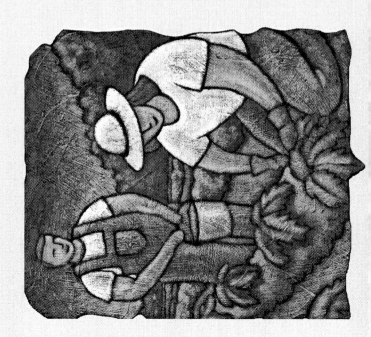

16

Every effort has been made to secure permission and provide appropriate credit for photographic material. The publisher deeply regrets any omission and pledges to correct errors called to its attention in subsequent editions.

Unless otherwise acknowledged, all photographs are the property of Scott Foresman, a division of Pearson Education.

Photo locators denoted as follows: Top (T), Center (C), Bottom (B), Left (L), Right (R), Background (Bkgd)

Illustrations by Nicole Wong

Photograph 16 Getty Images

ISBN: 0-328-13347-7

© Pearson Education, Inc.

Just before school started again, Kate said, "Let's pick our tomatoes before we get busy at school. They are red and ripe and ready to eat."

We invited Mayor Smith to help. The reporter who had followed the story of our garden was there too.

When we had finished our work, Mayor Smith took a big bite from a juicy red tomato. "Delicious!" he said with a smile. "Thank you!"

"Hooray for community spirit!" we cheered.

Every day on the way to school we walked by an empty lot. The grass was overgrown and littered with things people had thrown away. There were pieces of wood, empty bottles and cans, and old tires all over the ground. Years ago there had been a store there, but the store had closed and the building was torn down. Since then, no one had cared for the empty lot.

It rained for the next three days. Then on the fourth day we walked to the garden to see how things were growing. All our plants were in full bloom. The garden was more beautiful than ever.

Kate pointed to the tiny green tomatoes on the vines. "The tomatoes are growing so well!" she said proudly.

Jim collected beautiful flowers of every color for a bouquet.

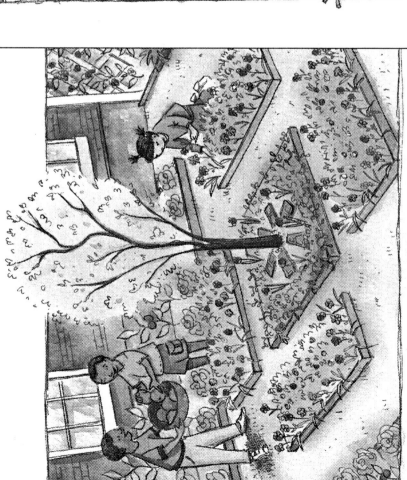

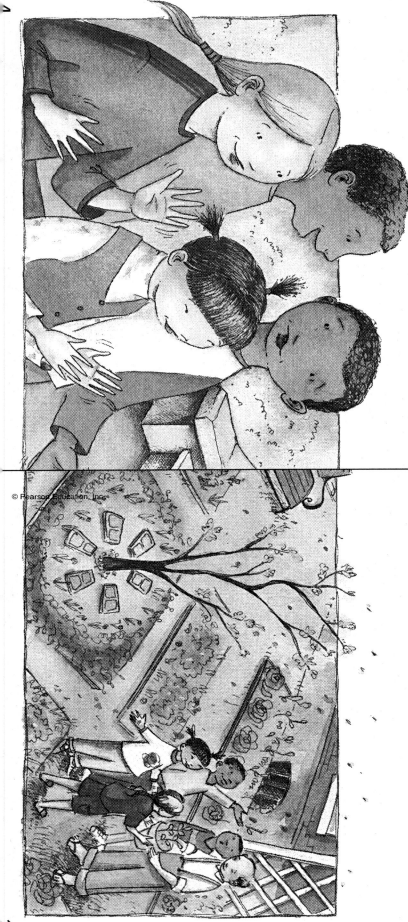

"All that litter makes our city look dirty," Kate said one day. "We could clean out that lot and make it a nice place for people to enjoy."

"We could turn it into a park!" said Jim.

"Or a basketball court!" said John.

Then I had an idea. "I know what we can do," I said. "We can plant a beautiful garden. That would give this old lot new life!"

"A garden?" asked my friends. "That's a great idea!" they agreed.

At the end of the summer our garden was finished. Everyone was thrilled with the change.

Mayor Smith came to dedicate the garden to the children of our city. "We all have a beautiful new garden to enjoy thanks to these great kids!" he announced. "Let's all do our part to give it the care it will need."

Suddenly, it began to rain. We all got soaked. But we smiled and laughed, knowing that the rain was great for our thirsty new garden!

We told our parents all about our idea. They were excited about our plan and wanted to help. They suggested that we go to City Hall and talk with the mayor of our city. He would know if we would be allowed to plant our garden on the empty lot.

The next day after school we all met with the mayor to discuss our plan. "That's a wonderful idea!" exclaimed Mayor Smith. "Children, you may begin work on your garden as soon as you'd like!" he told us excitedly.

The people of our city read about our garden and came to see it for themselves. "Amazing!" they said, as they admired the tomato vines. "Wonderful!" they exclaimed, as they walked around the tree.

Some people came to help. Mr. Yan brought a special plant for the garden. "It will bloom every year," he said.

Mr. and Mrs. Brown were experts at spotting weeds among the new plants.

Soon, summer vacation began. The weather was sunny and warm. We had plenty of free time, but we would not be lazy that summer. We were ready to begin our work at the old lot.

On the first day, we looked all around the lot to decide what needed to be done. "What a mess!" everybody said.

"Don't worry. We can clean this up," I said. It was a big job, but we were ready to work together as partners to clean up the lot.

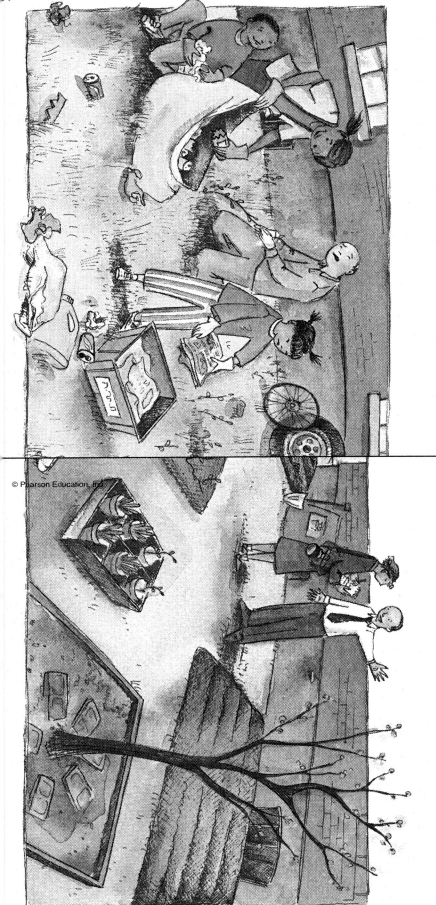

Each day, as we planted more of our garden, the empty lot became prettier.

One day, Mayor Smith brought a newspaper reporter to the lot. She was going to write a story about our garden for the city newspaper.

"These clever kids are bringing a wealth of community spirit to our city!" the mayor told her. "And you can quote me on that!"

The reporter talked with us and took our picture. We all held our shovels and smiled.

Jim picked up trash. Kate collected all the newspaper for recycling. We worked hard and did not cheat in our effort.

Our parents had their regular jobs to go to during the day. They didn't have much time to help us. But whenever they could they came by to pick up the sharp glass from broken bottles.

When Mayor Smith wasn't busy running the city, he came to help pull up weeds. "This old lot is looking great!" he exclaimed happily.

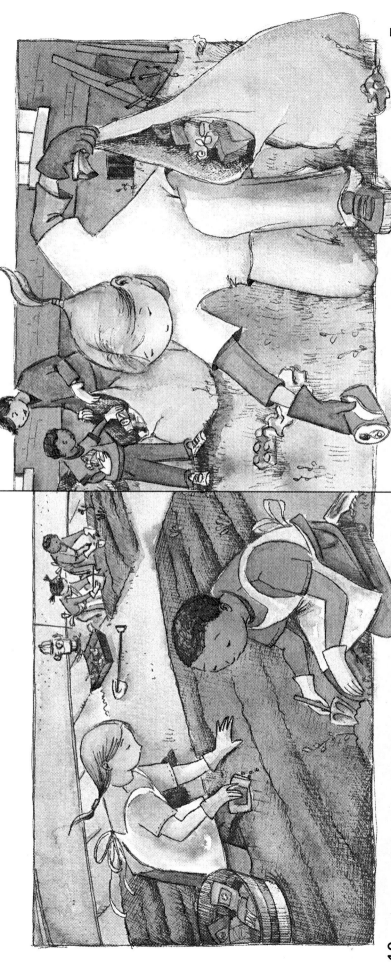

We worked in our garden almost every day of that summer vacation. We spread healthy soil across the lot to coat the ground. Then we carefully planted our flower seeds. Tiny tomato vines went in one corner. Our parents helped us plant a young tree right in the middle of the garden. Then we placed bricks around the bottom of the tree.

The hot sun made us sweat. We didn't mind though. We knew that the sunlight would help our plants and flowers grow.

7

Soon it was time to decide what we would plant in our garden. We all had good ideas.

"Let's plant crops of tomatoes and potatoes to eat," said Kate.

"I'd like to have blue and yellow and red and orange flowers," said Jim.

"It would be fun to have a big tree for climbing and reading in the shade," I said. "And we could build a treehouse after our tree grows!"

"If we plan carefully," said John, "we can make our garden exactly how we'd like it to be!"

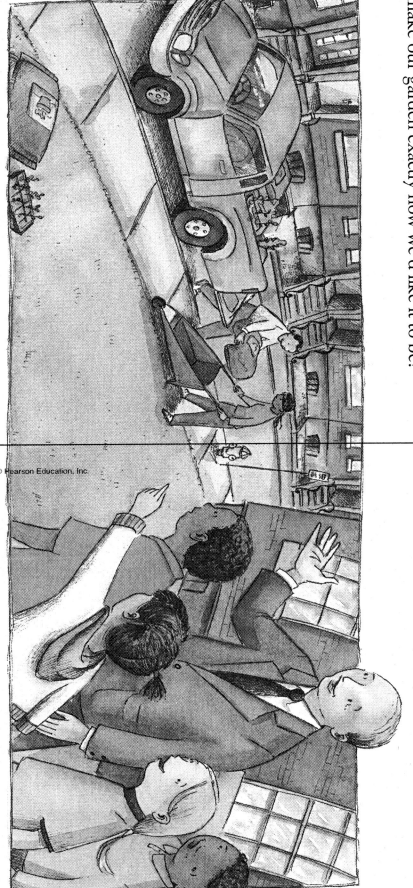

Later that day Mayor Smith and two other men arrived in a big truck. The truck was full of seeds and plants and soil for the garden.

"You are doing a wonderful thing for the people of our community," said the mayor. "The workers at City Hall have collected money to pay for the things you will need for the garden. It is a gift to you from our city!" he beamed.

We all cheered and thanked the mayor for his help.

The Colonial Adventure

by J. Matteson Claus • illustrated by Burgandy Beam

Suggested levels for Guided Reading, DRA,™
Lexile,® and Reading Recovery™ are provided
in the Pearson Scott Foresman Leveling Guide.

Genre	Comprehension Skills and Strategy	
Historical fiction	• Draw Conclusions • Setting • Ask Questions	

Scott Foresman Reading Street 3.2.5

PEARSON

Scott
Foresman

ISBN 0-328-13350-7

9 780328 133505

90000

Vocabulary

barrels

cellar

clearing

peg

spoil

steep

Word count: 1,007

Note: The total word count includes words in the running text and headings only.
Numerals and words in chapter titles, captions, labels, diagrams, charts, graphs,
sidebars, and extra features are not included.

Reader Response

1. What were the major differences between the Massachusetts and Virginia colonies?

2. Your English family is going to move to either colonial Massachusetts or Virginia. What questions would you ask Elizabeth and Sarah to help your family decide which colony to choose? Write your questions on a chart like the one below.

Ask Elizabeth	Ask Sarah

3. Use a dictionary to find three meanings of the word *spoil*. Then write *spoil* in three complete sentences to show the three different meanings.

4. After having read this book, do you think you would have chosen to start a new life in the colonies? Why or why not?

The Colonial Adventure

by J. Matteson Claus
illustrated by Burgandy Beam

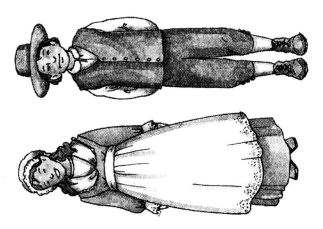

Editorial Offices: Glenview, Illinois • Parsippany, New Jersey • New York, New York
Sales Offices: Needham, Massachusetts • Duluth, Georgia • Glenview, Illinois
Coppell, Texas • Ontario, California • Mesa, Arizona

Did You Know?

The first permanent English settlement in North America was founded in Jamestown, Virginia, in the year 1607. Many of the settlers who came to Jamestown thought they would discover gold and silver there.

In 1630 the English Puritan settlers sailed into Massachusetts Bay and founded the city of Boston. The Puritans moved to Massachusetts to begin a new life where they could practice their religion freely.

Families in colonial times often lived in houses with only one room. It was called a keeping room. They cooked, ate, slept, and worked there.

In 1647 the Massachusetts Bay colony passed a law requiring every town with more than fifty families to have a school. Soon, other colonies adopted this law. Today in the United States, all children are required to go to school.

16

One night, at the beginning of the next winter, Elizabeth counted the months her family had been in Massachusetts. Twelve months had passed! Elizabeth was amazed as she thought about the exciting year it had been. She was happy in her new home.

Elizabeth picked up a pen and began to write to her cousin Sarah. She had a whole year of adventures to write about!

Elizabeth stood on the dock and looked at the huge ship. Her family was about to leave for their new home across the ocean. They were going to live in the New England colony called Massachusetts.

Elizabeth was eleven. It was her job to look after her five younger brothers and sisters. Elizabeth had never left England. She was nervous about the trip ahead. She and her family would start a whole new life in a land that they knew very little about.

Her brothers went with their father to help plant the farm. While the land in Jamestown was swampy, the Massachusetts soil was rocky. Instead of planting wheat and tobacco, Elizabeth's father planted fields of corn.

The colonists worked hard to learn what they could from the native people. They learned how to plant pumpkin, squash, and corn. They learned where to hunt and fish.

Soon Elizabeth and her family boarded the ship and began the long voyage to New England. Huge barrels of food and water had been brought aboard so they would have enough to eat during the trip. Still, there were many things that could go wrong while the ship was sailing on the open sea.

By the end of winter, Elizabeth's family was ready to move off the ship and into their new home. Now that they had a house to live in, the real work began. Each morning, Elizabeth went to school for a few hours in the village. There she practiced reading and writing. When Elizabeth returned home from school in the afternoon, she hung her coat on its peg and went to help her mother. She and her sisters helped with the cooking, cleaning, sewing, and, of course, the laundry. She was always busy. Keeping up with all the chores that needed to be done was hard!

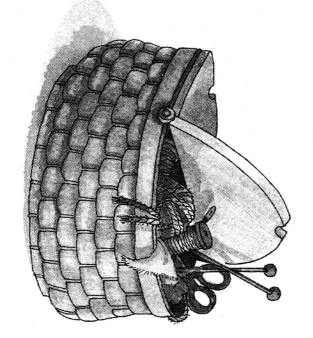

13

There was very little room on board the ship. The trip lasted for two months, and Elizabeth grew bored on the journey. To fight the boredom, she read letters she had kept from her cousin Sarah.

Sarah's family had moved to Jamestown, Virginia, a colony far to the south of Massachusetts. Elizabeth would have many of the same challenges that Sarah had written about in her letters.

OUR FARM

We have a farm now. Papa has begun growing wheat and a plant called tobacco. Already the crops have grown very high. We look forward to selling them!

Papa says your family will sail to the New World this autumn. Your new home in Massachusetts will be wonderful, I'm sure. We have heard about the forests, fish, and wildlife there.

Love,
Sarah

Elizabeth smiled, folded her letter carefully, and put it away.

Elizabeth smoothed open a letter and read:

Dear Cousin Elizabeth,

After many delays, we finally set sail in late January. It was a bumpy ocean crossing! There was a big storm in the middle of our voyage. All the grown-ups were very worried. Fortunately, we arrived safely in the Jamestown colony and started building our new home.

Jamestown
Our New
Home

OUR SHIP

England
Our Old
Home

During that long, cold winter, many people became sick. Even worse, there wasn't enough food to eat. Elizabeth was often hungry.

When she started to feel cold and hungry, Elizabeth took out her letters from Sarah. One of them began:

Dear Cousin,

Sometimes this New World can be difficult. The land here is very different from England. Jamestown is filled with swamps. It is not always easy to find clean, fresh water for drinking.

The people of our settlement are trying to make friends with the native people. There is little that they understand about us or that we understand about them. That makes talking with them difficult. Papa says that we should work with them and respect their ways.

Massachusetts
Your New Home X

Jamestown
Our New Home X

Everything here is so different, even the weather! You cannot imagine how hot the summers are in Virginia. They're worse than anything in England! We have to be careful that there is enough food and that none of it will spoil in the heat. To keep the food cool, we store as much of it as we can in the underground cellar.

I must go do my chores now. I promise to write again.

Your cousin,
Sarah

Soon her father came back. "I have found a clearing where we can build a new home," he said. "It's on top of a steep hill. There's a river close by with fresh water."

Elizabeth's mother hugged her husband. Elizabeth and her brothers and sisters began to shout and dance. A house of their very own! In England, Elizabeth's family had rented their house. In Massachusetts they would own their own farm!

It took several months to build the house. Elizabeth's family continued to live aboard the ship while they worked on the land.

Finally, the day arrived when their ship reached land. Elizabeth was excited. She couldn't wait to start her new life.

She stepped onto the ship's main deck and looked over the ship's railing. Elizabeth stared in wonder. Her new home was huge! The forest and fields stretched far into the distance. She could see a few houses peeking through the trees where the first colonists had settled.

"Come along, Elizabeth," her mother said. "There's work to be done." Now that they had arrived, the first thing that had to be done was the laundry! Their family and the other settlers had lived for two months aboard the ship without being able to clean their clothes.

Elizabeth and her brothers and sisters helped their mother with the washing. At the same time, Elizabeth's father went with the other men to look for land that would be good for settling.

Tulips
for Annie's Mother

by Peggy Bresnick Kendler

Suggested levels for Guided Reading, DRA,™
Lexile,® and Reading Recovery™ are provided
in the Pearson Scott Foresman Leveling Guide.

Genre	Comprehension Skills and Strategy
Historical fiction	• Cause and Effect • Author's Purpose • Story Structure

Scott Foresman Reading Street 3.3.1

ISBN 0-328-13353-1

9 780328 133536

90000

PEARSON

Scott
Foresman

Vocabulary

beauty

blooming

bulbs

doze

humor

recognizing

showers

sprouting

Word count: 781

Note: The total word count includes words in the running text and headings only. Numerals and words in chapter titles, captions, labels, diagrams, charts, graphs, sidebars, and extra features are not included.

Reader Response

1. At the beginning of the story, Annie's family is poor. Use a chart like the one below to show why and how life improves for the Borden family at the end of the story.

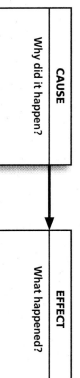

CAUSE	EFFECT
Why did it happen?	What happened?

2. Does this story take place in one day, or over many days? How do you know?

3. Here are three words that end in -ing: *recognizing, sprouting,* and *blooming.* Write sentences using each of these words.

4. How did people work together to help each other during the Great Depression?

Tulips for Annie's Mother

by Peggy Bresnick Kendler

illustrated by Robbie Short

Editorial Offices: Glenview, Illinois • Parsippany, New Jersey • New York, New York
Sales Offices: Needham, Massachusetts • Duluth, Georgia • Glenview, Illinois
Coppell, Texas • Ontario, California • Mesa, Arizona

The Great Depression

In October 1929, the stock market crashed. Many banks went out of business. People lost all the money they had saved in those banks. Rich people suddenly became poor. The following years were known as the Great Depression.

The Great Depression was a very tough time for people in the United States. Many people couldn't find any work. Some families lost their homes. They had to move away. Children stopped going to school. They did not have shoes or clothing to wear.

Many people in the United States were very poor at that time. Many shared what they could with others.

The Great Depression did not end until 1939.

ISBN: 0-328-13353-1

On the first nice day, Annie and her mother went out to plant the tulip bulbs. They dug small holes for the bulbs in the corner of the garden. "I'm so glad Dad found a job," said Annie.

Annie's mother smiled at her. "So am I," she said. "After spring showers, these bulbs will be sprouting and growing into tulips. Then we'll remember how lucky we are."

15

Annie Borden sat on the front porch. She was talking with her best friend, Sue. Sue's family was moving out of town. "I'll miss you," Sue said sadly.

"I'll miss you more," Annie said. She was afraid that her own family might have to move too. But she didn't tell Sue.

Annie gave Sue one last hug. She watched Sue walk home. She felt so sad.

Annie's father left for work early the next morning. This time, he was whistling. He would bring home 15 dollars every week. That was enough money to keep the family going. It was also enough money for both Annie and Tom to get new clothes.

Annie went inside her home. The house used to be toasty warm. Now it was cold. Annie wished she had some more sweaters to wear.

Life was not always like this. Two years ago, Annie had lots of clothes to wear. Her father still had his job. He worked as a bookkeeper. He brought money home every week. The family always had food. Annie and her older brother Tom had toys too.

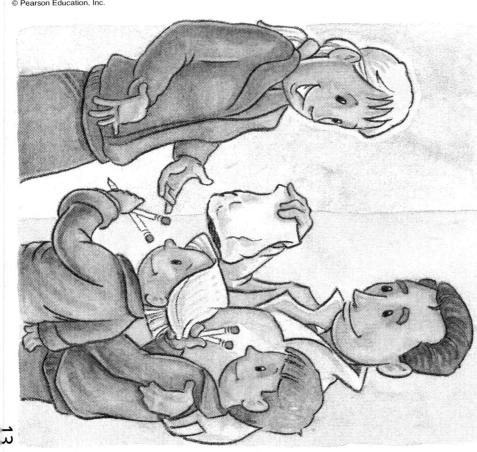

"Gifts for everyone!" said Annie's father. He handed the children new pencils. Then, he pulled out a small bag. "By spring, these should be blooming," he said.

Annie's mother opened the bag. Inside were tulip bulbs!

Everyone talked and joked as they ate dinner. It was the happiest day!

Annie remembered when everything changed. A year ago, in 1929, the stock market crashed. Annie's dad had told her about stocks. He said, "You could give money to a company to help run it. Then you owned a small part of that company. If the company made money, you made money too. If it didn't, then you didn't. But then suddenly, stocks were worth nothing. Banks were out of money. Rich people became poor people. Companies went out of business, and people lost their jobs." They called this time the Great Depression.

"I have a new job!" said Annie's father happily. "I am the new mechanic down at Hillson's Garage!"

Annie's mother looked at her husband. "A mechanic? Can you do that?" she asked.

"I fix our car. I know how engines work," he said. "To feed my family, I can do anything."

Sue was not the only one who had to move away. Her brother Tom's friend, Hank, moved to California to live with his aunt.

Tom had a job cleaning a neighbor's barn. He made a dollar a day. Annie tried to sell eggs by the road. But no one would buy them. Annie's father kept looking for work.

6

The next morning, Annie's father left early. "I'll get bread today," he said. Annie knew that the bread lines were very long. Often more than a hundred people would stand in line to get free food. It could take hours before her father got home!

Annie and Tom were about to doze off, when their father came home. He was smiling!

11

Annie's mother looked sadly out the window. "This is the first year I won't plant tulips. There's no money to buy bulbs," Annie's mother said.

Annie felt very sad. She knew how much her mother loved the beauty of the flowers.

Annie ran to open the door. She recognized their friend, Mr. Rice. Mr. Rice didn't live on a farm. Annie's mother knew he was hungry. She often invited him and his family to dinner. "My wife knit this blanket," he said. Annie's mother took the blanket. She handed Mr. Rice two bottles of milk. "Will you stay for dinner?" she asked. "Another time, Mrs. Borden," he said. "Thanks."

Just then, Annie's father came home. "Dad!" Annie called out. Annie's father used to have a great sense of humor. Now he hardly ever smiled.

"Any luck?" asked Annie's mother. Annie's father shook his head. Every day, he looked for work. He waited outside buildings where people might give out jobs. There was always a crowd of men.

Annie's family sat down to dinner. "At least we have corn and potatoes from our farm," Annie's mother said. "We have fresh milk from our cows. What we can't sell, we can keep for us. We're lucky we live on a farm."

Just then, there was a knock on the door.

Earth Science

Science

Science

Pictures in the Sky

by Chanelle Peters

Genre	Comprehension Skills and Strategy	Text Features
Expository nonfiction	• Author's Purpose • Main Idea • Summarize	• Captions • Labels • Diagrams • Glossary

Scott Foresman Reading Street 3.3.2

ISBN 0-328-13356-6

90000

9 780328 133567

PEARSON

Scott
Foresman

Vocabulary

antlers

imagined

language

narrator

overhead

poke

Word count: 698

Note: The total word count includes words in the running text and headings only.
Numerals and words in chapter titles, captions, labels, diagrams, charts, graphs,
sidebars, and extra features are not included.

Reader Response

1. Why do you think the author wrote this book?

2. Summarize what happened in 1928 when the astronomers from different countries met (see page 6). Use a graphic organizer like the one below.

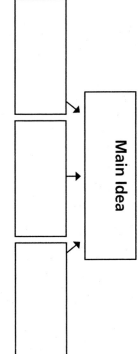

Main Idea

3. One of the Glossary words is a compound, made up of two separate words. Which word is it? Use it in a sentence.

4. The constellations Aries and Delphinus are shown on pages 6 and 7. Do you think they look like the pictures of the ram and the dolphin shown next to them? Why or why not?

Pictures in the Sky

by Chanelle Peters

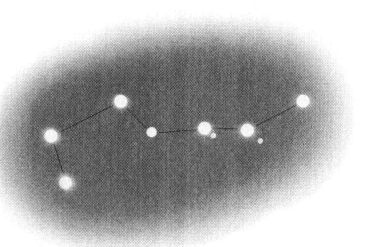

PEARSON
Scott Foresman

Editorial Offices: Glenview, Illinois • Parsippany, New Jersey • New York, New York
Sales Offices: Needham, Massachusetts • Duluth, Georgia • Glenview, Illinois
Coppell, Texas • Ontario, California • Mesa, Arizona

Glossary

antlers *n.* bony growths on the heads of deer, elk, and moose that are shed each year. Antlers grow in pairs, and branch out. They are like horns.

imagined *v.* to have pictured something in your mind or formed an image or idea of it.

language *n.* human speech, spoken or written.

narrator *n.* a person who tells a story.

overhead *adv.* something you have to look up to see.

poke *v.* to push against with something pointed.

16

Every effort has been made to secure permission and provide appropriate credit for photographic material. The publisher deeply regrets any omission and pledges to correct errors called to its attention in subsequent editions.

Unless otherwise acknowledged, all photographs are the property of Scott Foresman, a division of Pearson Education.

Photo locators denoted as follows: Top (T), Center (C), Bottom (B), Left (L), Right (R), Background (Bkgd)

Opener: Brand X Pictures, (c)Dorling Kindersley; 1 (c)Dorling Kindersley; 3 (c)Dorling Kindersley; 4 (c)Dorling Kindersley; 5 Brand X Pictures; 6 (BL) (c)Dorling Kindersley, (CR) Getty Images; 7 (B)(c)Dorling Kindersley, (CR) Corbis; 9 (c)Dorling Kindersley; 10 (c)Dorling Kindersley; 11 (c)Dorling Kindersley; 12 (c)Dorling Kindersley; 13 (c)Dorling Kindersley; 14 (c)Dorling Kindersley; 15 (c)Dorling Kindersley

ISBN: 0-328-13356-6

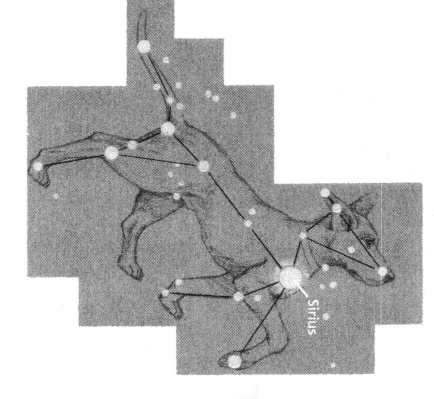

The star Sirius is part of the constellation Canis Major.

Sirius

You've now learned plenty about the constellations. Think about what you've learned the next time you look at the night sky. You might be able to recognize the constellations talked about in this book!

When was the last time you looked up at the night sky? Have you ever wanted to **poke** your finger through the stars in the night sky? If so, you are like the ancient astronomers. They lived thousands of years ago. They spent their time gazing at the stars.

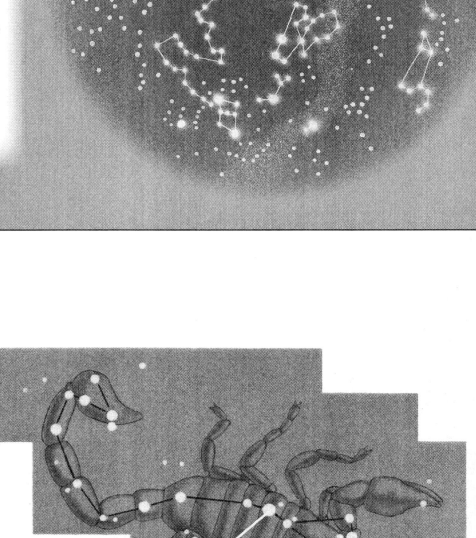

Native Americans tell a tale about the stars Sirius and Antares. They call them the Dog Stars. The **narrator** explains that when people die they travel through the sky. Then they have to pass the Dog Stars. If they feed only the first dog and not the second one, they will be stuck in the night sky forever.

The star Antares is part of the constellation Scorpius.

Antares

Ancient astronomers **imagined** that there were lines between some stars. To them the lines made shapes and patterns. These patterns became known as constellations. Each constellation has its own area of the sky. Many constellations were named after gods and heroes from Greek and Roman myths. People also liked to name constellations after animals.

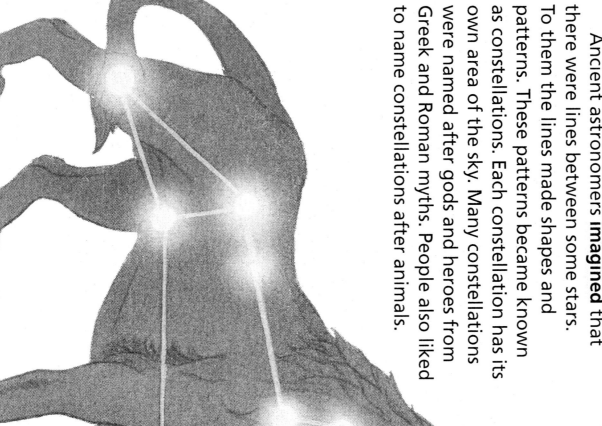

To people who lived in Africa, the cluster of stars called Pleiades was very important. One group of Africans, the Bantu people, believed Pleiades represented a plow. When the Bantu people saw Pleiades in the sky, it was time for them to begin plowing and planting crops.

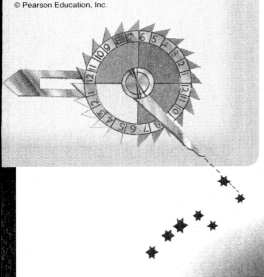

At different times of the year you you can see different constellations in the sky. You may find it hard to see a shape in a constellation. That's because constellations only suggest things. They don't show actual people or animals. The stars in a constellation make up the outline of a shape or object. People have to fill in the outline using their imagination and what they have heard about the constellation.

The stars that make up the constellation Leo.

The ancient Egyptians also watched the stars. One of their most important stars was the star we call Sirius. Once a year just before sunrise, Sirius can be seen in Egypt. When the ancient Egyptians saw Sirius, they took it as a sign that the Nile River would flood. Without those floods, Egyptian farmers could not grow their crops. So when an Egyptian farmer saw Sirius, he or she would be hopeful.

An Egyptian stairwell, with a gauge for measuring Nile River floods (right), and a star clock (far right).

The astronomers of ancient Mesopotamia were the first to name constellations. Astronomers of ancient Egypt and Greece also named constellations. The first star charts had forty-eight constellations.

In 1928 astronomers from around the world met. They decided to organize the night stars. The astronomers placed the stars into separate constellations. They created eighty-eight constellations.

The constellation Hercules

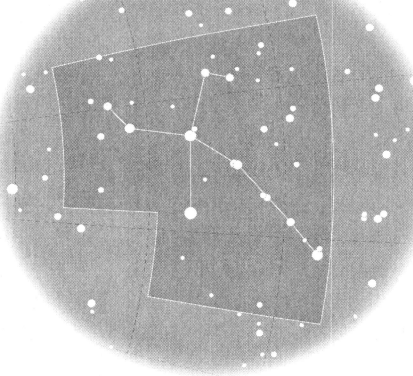

The Greeks and Romans spent many nights looking **overhead** at the night sky. Greek and Roman parents would point out constellations such as Hercules to their children. They would tell stories about this hero's great strength while looking at his constellation.

The eighty-eight constellations were given Latin names. Some you might know. One of the constellations is called Aries. Aries means "ram." A ram is a male sheep. Rams have horns. Horns are like **antlers.** Delphinus, another constellation, means "dolphin." Why do these names come from the Latin **language?** Because people who spoke Latin discovered and named many constellations.

Aries, which means "ram" (below left), and Delphinus, which means "dolphin" (below right)

The Greeks and Romans had many great astronomers. They gave names to many different stars and constellations. The word *astronomy* comes from Greek words meaning "star" and "law." The ancient Greeks and Romans used constellations to honor their gods, such as Juno and Zeus.

A statue of Juno (above), and a statue of Zeus (left)

Some constellations have very bright stars. These bright stars were important to ancient peoples. They gave them names.

Most of these stars have Greek or Arabic names. The constellation Gemini contains the stars Castor and Pollux. Those names are Greek. It also contains the stars Wasat, Mebsuta, and Alhena. Those names are Arabic.

You have already read about the names of the constellations. The constellations also have stories. These stories are taken from African, Chinese, Egyptian, Greek, Roman, and Native American mythology.

A myth is an old story that has been told orally for generations. Myths often explain how things in nature came to be. Other stories tell about amazing events involving gods and heroes.

An ancient Roman temple built to honor Castor and Pollux

The First Year

by Christian Downey
illustrated by Tom McNeely

Genre	Comprehension Skills and Strategy	
Historical fiction	• Draw Conclusions • Plot • Ask Questions	

Scott Foresman Reading Street 3.3.3

ISBN 0-328-13359-0

9 780328 133598

90000

PEARSON

Scott
Foresman

Vocabulary

blade

budding

dew

fireflies

flutter

hawkmoth

notepad

patch

Word count: 922

Note: The total word count includes words in the running text and headings only. Numerals and words in chapter titles, captions, labels, diagrams, charts, graphs, sidebars, and extra features are not included.

Reader Response

1. If the settlers' crops grew badly one year, what could you conclude about that year's weather? What if the crops grew well? Use a graphic organizer like the one below to help show your conclusions.

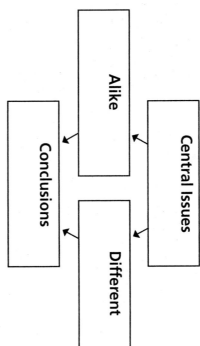

2. Imagine you could talk to Jacob and Sarah about their experiences. What would you ask them?

3. *Notepad* is a compound word. What two smaller words make it up? Think of other compound words using *note* and still others using *pad*.

4. Jacob and Sarah moved to a new country. How would you feel if you moved to a new place? Why?

The First Year

by Christian Downey
illustrated by Tom McNeely

PEARSON
Scott Foresman

Editorial Offices: Glenview, Illinois • Parsippany, New Jersey • New York, New York
Sales Offices: Needham, Massachusetts • Duluth, Georgia • Glenview, Illinois
Coppell, Texas • Ontario, California • Mesa, Arizona

Edible Plants

Some birds and insects feed on the nectar found in plants and flowers. People also rely on plants for nourishment.

Not all plants and flowers are safe to eat. Some can be eaten raw, and others must be cooked. Some plants get sprayed with unsafe chemicals. Others may have dangerous growths. Experts know how to identify wild or dangerous plants. They stay away from plants that are bitter and those with spines or thorns. It is safe to eat plants that blossom into food, such as strawberries, pumpkins, and tomatoes.

Certain plants, like mistletoe, are not safe to eat. Other plants, like ripe tomatoes on a vine, provide food for people.

16

Every effort has been made to secure permission and provide appropriate credit for photographic material. The publisher deeply regrets any omission and pledges to correct errors called to its attention in subsequent editions.

Unless otherwise acknowledged, all photographs are the property of Scott Foresman, a division of Pearson Education.

Photo locators denoted as follows: Top (T), Center (C), Bottom (B), Left (L), Right (R), Background (Bkgd)

Opener: Illustrations by Tom McNeely

Photographs 16 ©DK Images

ISBN: 0-328-13359-0

All of the settlers came to the feast. Their Native American friends came too. People brought bread, meat, cakes, and pies. They made everything themselves. Everyone shared. Jacob and Sarah ate the cake they made. When the feast ended, they went home to bed. Jacob and Sarah were thankful for their new home.

15

Chapter One

Jacob and Sarah arrived in Virginia with their parents in the early spring of 1630. They came on a large ship with many other families. The new land would be their home. Along with the others, they hoped to build a colony. It was a big change for them. Jacob and Sarah liked the open land. They wanted to explore and see new things.

Chapter Five

Jacob and Sarah had been working hard. They'd been working too hard to notice that fall was almost over! Winter was now not far off. One day, Jacob and Sarah's mother woke them early.

"Jacob! Sarah! Wake up! Today is the feast!" she said.

The settlers had been in Virginia for three full seasons. To celebrate, they decided to have a big feast. Jacob and Sarah helped their mother make a cake. When the cake was done, they cooled it on the windowsill. They walked to the big barn with their parents.

First they had to build. Jacob and Sarah's father helped build barns and cabins.

"Father, can we help too?" asked Jacob.

"Yes, Father. What can we do?" asked Sarah.

"You can help find logs. Look in the forest for trees and fallen logs. We can make houses and boats out of them," said their father.

"Let's go, Sarah!" said Jacob.

Jacob and Sarah walked to the nearby woods.

"It's pointing to the right," Sarah said.

"Which way did it point last night before the rain came?" asked Jacob.

"Last night it pointed to the left," said Sarah.

"So when it points left, rain might be coming!" said Jacob.

They ran home to tell their father. He would be happy that they helped.

Chapter Four

In order to make their own weather vane, Jacob and Sarah first found a piece of rope. They hung the rope over the branch of a small tree that grew in their mother's garden. Then they tied a pointed piece of wood to the end of the rope. When the weather was good, they marked places in the dirt to show which way their weather vane pointed.

One rainy and windy day, they went out to the garden. "Sarah, which way is the wood pointing?" asked Jacob.

Jacob and Sarah found many big trees and fallen logs. Their father and a few other men used them to build a new boat.

It was still early spring, so the weather was still cold. To help keep them warm, Jacob and Sarah's father made fires from the logs.

Jacob and Sarah's father also used the wood to make a gift. He sliced the wood thin, like paper, and sewed together the pages to make notepads. Father made one notepad for Jacob and another for Sarah.

Chapter Two

Spring came. The weather got warm and the ground thawed. Dew sparkled on the grass outside in the mornings. Jacob and Sarah's mother planted flowers in a garden next to their small house.

Jacob and Sarah liked to help their mother in the garden. Sarah helped put the seeds in the ground. Jacob watered them.

One day, their mother called them outside. "Sarah! Jacob! Come look!" she said.

Summer came and went. Soon it was early fall. The nights started getting colder again. When the frost came, the settlers tried to protect the crops and land.

To help predict what kind of weather might be coming, Jacob and Sarah's father had made a weather vane out of wood. He had cut the wood carefully with the blade of a knife.

Jacob and Sarah's father had placed the weather vane on top of the barn. It told them which way the wind blew. Jacob and Sarah loved to watch the weather vane twist and turn in the wind. They wanted to have their own!

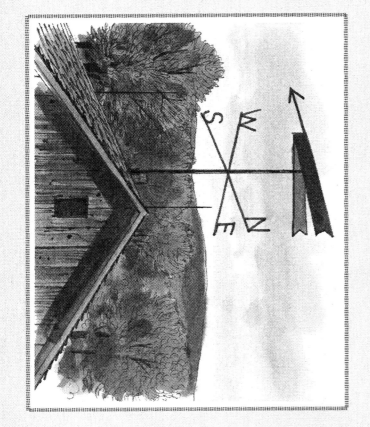

The seeds that Sarah and Jacob had planted were now budding into flowers.

"It's growing! We did it!" said Jacob.

"Let's plant more!" said Sarah.

All through the spring, Sarah and Jacob helped their mother plant more flowers. Soon, the garden was blooming with every color!

It had been raining for several days. Now that it was summer, the rain was warm. Jacob and Sarah did not like the many days of rain. They had to stay inside when the rains came.

Sarah and Jacob looked out the window at the patch of land where their garden grew.

"Jacob, when will the rain end?" asked Sarah.

"Soon, I hope. But at least the berries will grow!" said Jacob.

Their mother was growing blueberries and strawberries. She would make pies when they were ready.

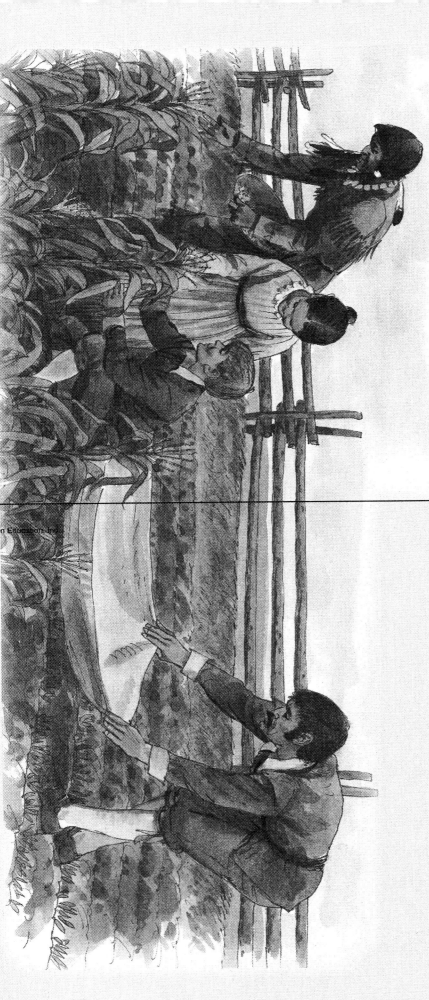

The weather got much warmer as summer got closer. Fireflies came out at night to flutter all around the houses. Soon, the settlers were able to grow vegetables to eat. Native Americans who lived nearby showed them how. The settlers planted seeds to grow corn, squash, beans, and other crops. Jacob and Sarah liked to check on the vegetables.

Chapter Three

The settlers gave the Native Americans tools for cooking. They traded items. The settlers and the Native Americans each had things that could help the other. Jacob and Sarah were thankful. They liked the vegetables that the Native Americans helped them plant.

A Day With the Dogs

by Rena Korb

Illustrated by CD Hullinger

Suggested levels for Guided Reading, DRA,™
Lexile,® and Reading Recovery™ are provided
in the Pearson Scott Foresman Leveling Guide.

Genre	Comprehension Skills and Strategy	
Realistic fiction	• Generalize • Character • Answer Questions	

Scott Foresman Reading Street 3.3.4

ISBN 0-328-13362-0

9 780328 133628

90000

Vocabulary

anxiously

bay

blizzard

channel

chip

melody

supplies

surrounded

symphony

Word count: 1,037

Reader Response

1. What services do animal rescue shelters provide to the community? Use a graphic organizer like the one below to help you make a list.

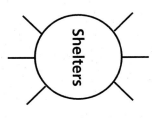

Shelters

2. How did Dr. Tran and Dana's mom take care of the puppy that Dana found in the parking lot?

3. On page 15, the author uses the word *anxiously*. Why was that word used there?

4. Why was the stray dog's identification chip so important to Dr. Tran? What might have happened if the dog didn't have the chip?

A Day With the Dogs

by Rena Korb

illustrated by
CD Hullinger

PEARSON

Scott
Foresman

Editorial Offices: Glenview, Illinois • Parsippany, New Jersey • New York, New York
Sales Offices: Needham, Massachusetts • Duluth, Georgia • Glenview, Illinois
Coppell, Texas • Ontario, California • Mesa, Arizona

Seeing Eye Dogs

Many people who are blind depend on dogs to serve as guides. Seeing Eye dogs help their owners get around safely at home and in the world.

Seeing Eye dogs lead their owners around obstacles and across streets. They stop for cars coming out of driveways, and they warn their owners about staircases!

With Seeing Eye dogs, people who are blind can travel in busy cities and even ride on the subway. Seeing Eye dogs help keep their owners safe.

16

ISBN: 0-328-13362-0

Copyright © Pearson Education, Inc.

All Rights Reserved. Printed in the United States of America. This publication is protected by Copyright, and permission should be obtained from the publisher prior to any prohibited reproduction, storage in a retrieval system, or transmission in any form by any means, electronic, mechanical, photocopying, recording, or likewise. For information regarding permission(s), write to: Permissions Department, Scott Foresman, 1900 East Lake Avenue, Glenview, Illinois 60025.

2 3 4 5 6 7 8 9 10 V0G1 14 13 12 11 10 09 08 07 06 05

Dana watched anxiously as Dr. Tran picked up the office telephone. He said, "I'm going to try the owners now."

Dana listened as Dr. Tran explained how she and her mom had found the dog. To her surprise, he held the phone out to her.

"We want to thank you so much for finding Inky," a woman's voice said. "We're going to come pick him up right now."

What a day! Dana thought, relieved. She couldn't wait to see what would happen next week at the shelter!

"Dana! Wake up!" Dana opened her eyes to see her mother leaning over the bed. "The animal rescue shelter called. A bad snowstorm is on the way. They expect the volunteers to bring in a lot of stray dogs today. Do you want to come to the shelter with me to help out?"

Without a word, Dana sat up and jumped out of bed.

"That's what I thought you'd say," laughed her mother.

Dana looked at the dog more closely. "He doesn't look like a stray, but he's not wearing a collar," she said. "I bet his owners miss him."

"Then let's see if we can find them," Dr. Tran said. He pulled out a small wand. "This scanner checks for an identification chip buried under the skin." The scanner beeped loudly as it passed over the puppy's neck.

"The chip has the animal's special code number on it," Dana's mom explained. "We can use the number to find out who owns this puppy."

Dana had recently begun volunteering at the animal rescue shelter where her mom worked as a veterinarian. The shelter was just across the bay from their house.

Dana was learning many different jobs at the shelter. She fed the dogs and cleaned their cages. She played catch with the dogs in the shelter's backyard. Dana's favorite job, however, was introducing people to the dogs waiting for adoption. Whenever a dog found a new home, Dana was especially pleased!

Dr. Tran looked up as the doorbell rang. It jingled in a pretty melody. Most of the time, Dana liked the sound of the doorbell. Now she was too busy to notice it.

Dana watched as her mom and Dr. Tran rushed to care for the puppy. The two veterinarians wrapped him in warm towels and rubbed him softly. The dog slowly raised his head. Then he barked.

Dr. Tran quickly examined the dog. "He's going to be OK. Dana, you saved his life!"

The road to the shelter crossed over the bay. Dana looked for boats in the channel, but there were none. Dana's mom turned on the radio to listen to the news as they drove. The weather reporter announced that a blizzard might hit some parts of the state.

Dana looked at the sky. "Will we get a blizzard here?" she asked.

"We don't usually get blizzards," her mom said, "but it will get very cold and snowy."

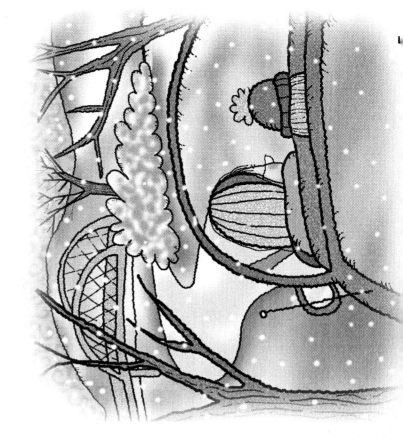

Dana and her mom walked through the cold parking lot. Suddenly Dana heard a noise and noticed movement in the snow. There was something behind the shelter's dumpster!

"Mom, look!" Dana cried and pointed. It was a black dog with white patches, curled up into a ball. The dog was so small that Dana had trouble seeing it.

Dana's mom carefully picked up the puppy. Then she and Dana hurried back to the shelter.

Dana forgot about the snowstorm as soon as she entered the animal shelter. "Hi, Dr. Tran," Dana said. "Hi, Maria." Dana worked with Dr. Tran and Maria. They had taught her a lot about dogs already.

"Hi, Dana," Dr. Tran said. "I'm very glad to see you. We need all the help we can get today."

Maria said, "Since it's going to be so busy, I'm putting you in charge of taking care of the dogs. Do you think you can handle it?"

"Oh, yes!" Dana exclaimed.

Maria gently took her arm. "I could use your help again," she said. In the supply room, Maria turned on the stereo. The notes of a symphony filled the room.

Dana and Maria got to work putting away the supplies of dog food and treats. Dana scooped freshly chipped wood for the dogs' play area into a wheelbarrow. Together, Maria and Dana met with people who had arrived hoping to find new pets.

The rest of the morning flew by. When it was time to go home, Dana was so tired that she couldn't stop yawning.

11

After Dana had finished visiting with the dogs, she went back to the office area. She wondered what else she could do to help. The door to the veterinarian's office had swung open. Inside, Dana's mother and Dr. Tran moved from dog to dog. Some dogs barked loudly. Others whined and whimpered. Dana stood in the doorway and stared. She had never seen so many sick dogs.

Maria and Dana started down the long hall to the kennel area. As they walked, Dana heard loud wailing noises. She knew they were coming from the dogs.

"Why are the dogs crying like that?" she asked. "I've never heard them sound so sad."

"Animals often sense changes in the weather," Maria answered. "This is their way of telling us they don't like it one bit!"

When the dogs saw Dana they became quiet. Many of them raced to the front of their cages to greet her. Stumpy led the pack. He had lost his front leg in a fight, but he ran just as quickly as the other dogs. Butterfly stuck her nose through the bars. Her pink tongue darted out of her mouth to lick Dana's hand. *It is nice to be surrounded by so many friends*, Dana thought.

Dana stepped into each cage. She poured fresh food and water into the bowls. Then she spent several minutes cuddling each dog.

Dana decided to spend extra time with the new puppy, Elvis. Elvis was very shy around people. Dana used a dog treat to coax him out of his corner. "You don't have to be afraid," she crooned. Soon Elvis came to sit on her lap. Dana knew that when Elvis left the shelter, she would miss him the most.

Earth Science

Mount St. Helens

by Isabel Sendao

Science

Science

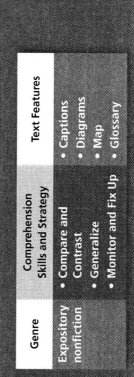

Genre	Comprehension Skills and Strategy	Text Features
Expository nonfiction	• Compare and Contrast • Generalize • Monitor and Fix Up	• Captions • Diagrams • Map • Glossary

Scott Foresman Reading Street 3.3.5

ISBN 0-328-13365-5

9 780328 133659

90000

PEARSON

Scott
Foresman

Vocabulary

beneath

buried

chimney

earthquakes

fireworks

force

tremble

volcano

Word count: 782

Reader Response

1. Some parts of Mount St. Helens got hit with landslides. Other parts got hit with lava flows. Use a graphic organizer like the one below to compare and contrast how life has returned to these two areas.

Hit with landslides	Hit with lava flows

2. Reread the section on page 9 that describes how Mount St. Helens' bulge exploded. Where in the book did you first read about a bulge?

3. The word *tremble* is used on page 6. Use the word *tremble* in a sentence that talks about a living thing.

4. What were you able to learn about the Cascades from the map on page 3?

Mount St. Helens

by Isabel Sendao

Editorial Offices: Glenview, Illinois • Parsippany, New Jersey • New York, New York
Sales Offices: Needham, Massachusetts • Duluth, Georgia • Glenview, Illinois
Coppell, Texas • Ontario, California • Mesa, Arizona

Glossary

beneath *adv.* in a lower place; below; underneath; under.

buried *v.* to be covered up by something.

chimney *n.* an upright structure of brick or stone that carries away smoke.

earthquakes *n.* shaking or shifting motions of Earth's surface.

fireworks *n.* firecrackers, rockets, etc., that make loud noises or beautiful, fiery displays.

force *n.* active power or strength.

tremble *v.* to move in short, jerky movements; to shake.

volcano *n.* opening in Earth's crust through which steam, ashes, and lava are forced out in periods of activity.

There is now a monument on Mount St. Helens. It reminds us of the eruption of 1980. Observation stations have been placed on and around the mountain. They let people see how Mount St. Helens has changed since the eruption.

Mount St. Helens has erupted a few times since 1980. It will continue to erupt in the future. Still, with plenty of warning, no one should be hurt. So people will keep watching for signs of trouble!

Copyright © Pearson Education, Inc.

ISBN: 0-328-13365-5

Opener: Getty Images; 3 (B) Getty Images, (R) Digital Wisdom, Inc.; 4 Getty Images; 5 Getty Images; 6 (c)Dorling Kindersley; 7 (c)Dorling Kindersley; 8 (c)Dorling Kindersley; 9 Getty Images; 11 (c)Dorling Kindersley; 12 (CL) (c)Dorling Kindersley, (B) Getty Images; 13 Getty Images; 14 (c)Dorling Kindersley; 15 Getty Images

Photo locators denoted as follows: Top (T), Center (C), Bottom (B), Left (L), Right (R), Background (Bkgd)

Unless otherwise acknowledged, all photographs are the property of Scott Foresman, a division of Pearson Education.

Every effort has been made to secure permission and provide appropriate credit for photographic material. The publisher deeply regrets any omission and pledges to correct errors called to its attention in subsequent editions.

2 3 4 5 6 7 8 9 10 V0G1 14 13 12 11 10 09 08 07 06 05

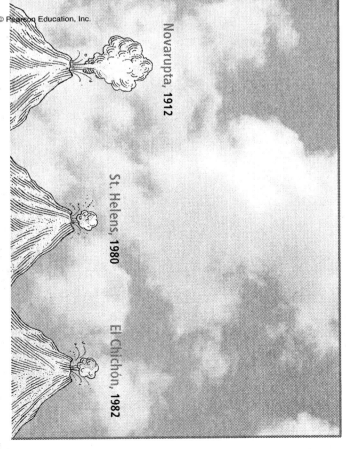

Novarupta, 1912

St. Helens, 1980

El Chichón, 1982

Mount St. Helens is a **volcano**. It is located in Washington State. Mount St. Helens is part of the Cascade mountain range. The Cascades go through northern California, Oregon, and Washington State.

The Cascades include Mount Rainier, Mount Shasta, and Mount Hood. But Mount St. Helens is as famous as those others. It is famous for what happened on May 18, 1980.

The Cascades extend for hundreds of miles.

The Mount St. Helens eruption of 1980 was one of the biggest in United States history. It taught scientists many things about volcanoes. They learned about how a volcano acts before it erupts. They also gained a lot of information to help them predict when other volcanoes might erupt. Scientists have used this information to study how volcanoes affect the land around them.

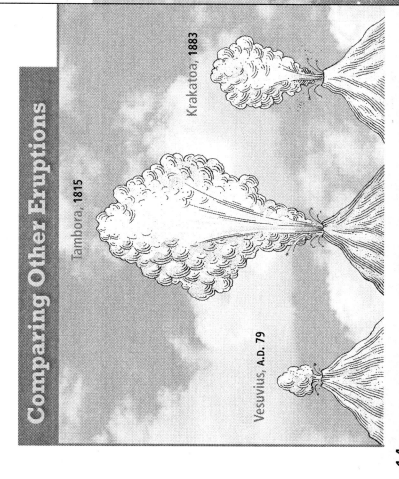

Comparing Other Eruptions

Tambora, 1815

Krakatoa, 1883

Vesuvius, A.D. 79

Mount St. Helens' Spirit Lake (above), the mountain's crater giving off smoke and ash (right).

Before then Mount St. Helens had been a popular place for outdoor activities. Its lake, Spirit Lake, always had lots of visitors. Not many of those visitors realized that the mountain sitting just above them was an active volcano.

Some of the plants and trees are growing more slowly than others. Where there were lava flows, the plants and trees have barely begun to grow back. But where there were only mudslides, the trees and plants are growing faster. Scientists estimate it will take more than two hundred years for the plant life of Mount St. Helens to completely grow back.

Animals are also coming back. Since there are more plants and trees now, there is more for the animals to eat.

On May 18, 1980, Mount St. Helens erupted. The mountain's last eruption had been in 1857. At that time what we now call Washington State was not even a state! The land that is now Washington State was admitted into the United States in 1889.

The volcano continued to tremble and erupt for weeks after the first eruption. Small earthquakes shook the mountain frequently. But the worst part of the eruption was over.

More than twenty-five years have passed since the eruption of 1980. The forest on and below Mount St. Helens is slowly growing back.

Volcanic rock (left), Mount St. Helens (below), and a mountain meadow near Mount St. Helens (right)

Mount St. Helens had been giving off warning signs throughout early 1980. Those signs made scientists believe an eruption was likely.

Many small **earthquakes** shook the volcano. Lava inside the volcano built up pressure. The **force** from that pressure created a bulge in the volcano. The pressure also caused the volcano to **tremble**.

Can you see the rivers of lava coming down the side of this volcano?

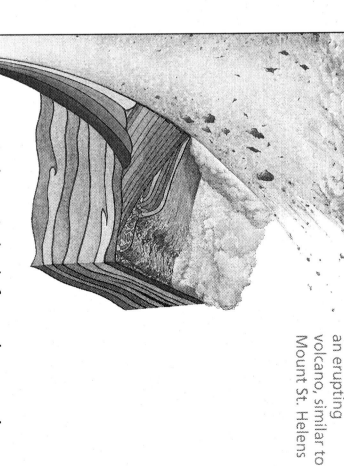

A diagram showing an erupting volcano, similar to Mount St. Helens

Winds carried ash from the eruption many miles to the east. The ash covered the city of Yakima, Washington in a thick cloud. It was heavy enough to collapse roofs. People had to wear masks to help them breathe. It took many weeks to clean up all the ash that fell on the city.

Scientists monitored the mountain carefully. They wanted to make sure that everyone around Mount St. Helens would be safe in case of an eruption. The scientists studied the small earthquakes created by the mountain. They also monitored the steam and gas that rose from the mountain.

Scientists use devices like this theodolite to detect changes in a volcano's shape.

Park rangers did their best to make sure that people got away in time. Most people listened to the rangers. But a man named Harry Truman, who had the same name as the former United States president, refused to leave. Truman saw the mountain as his home. When it erupted, Harry and his house were buried under tons of mud.

The rock and ash from the eruption rained like **fireworks**. Nearly 230 square miles of forest were destroyed. The eruption also made a crater, or shallow hole.

The scientists spent a lot of time watching the bulge. It grew every day. Its growth made the scientists nervous. They knew that only a huge amount of pressure could cause such a bulge. The pressure and the bulge it made scared the scientists more than any other warning sign.

Six Stages of a Volcano

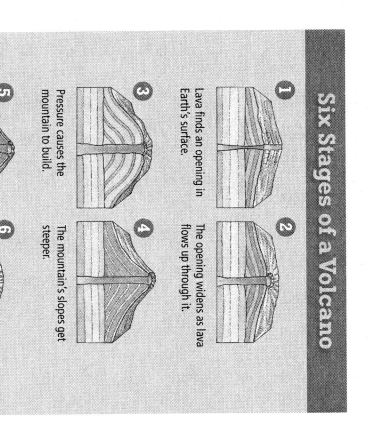

1 Lava finds an opening in Earth's surface.

2 The opening widens as lava flows up through it.

3 Pressure causes the mountain to build.

4 The mountain's slopes get steeper.

5 Side vents form inside the volcano.

6 The volcano may erupt, blasting out a huge crater.

Finally, after weeks of giving off warning signs, Mount St. Helens erupted.

The bulge at the top of the volcano exploded. It went sliding down into Spirit Lake. The bulge's explosion reduced the mountain's height by more than one thousand feet.

Lava flows raced down the mountain's slopes. The mountain smoked like a **chimney**. Trees and plants were **buried beneath** ash and rock. After nine hours, the eruption finally ended.

BRAVE SETTLERS IN A STRANGE LAND

by Donna Foley

illustrated by Ron Mahoney

Suggested levels for Guided Reading, DRA,™
Lexile,® and Reading Recovery™ are provided
in the Pearson Scott Foresman Leveling Guide.

Genre	Comprehension Skills and Strategy	Text Features
Narrative nonfiction	• Cause and Effect • Author's Purpose • Answer Questions	• Chart • Captions • Glossary

Scott Foresman Reading Street 3.4.1

ISBN 0-328-13368-X

9 780328 133680

90000

Reader Response

1. Reread page 12. Why were many of the immigrants frightened when they came to Ellis Island? Use a graphic organizer like the one below to show what happened and why.

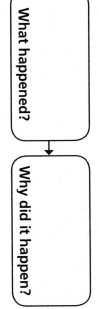

What happened? → Why did it happen?

2. Why has America been called a *melting pot*? Where did you find the answer?

3. Write an interesting sentence using the word *drifting*.

4. How would you feel about leaving your home to start a new life in a strange land?

Vocabulary

attention
complained
drifting
giggle
glaring
looping
struggled
swooping

Word count: 1,013

Note: The total word count includes words in the running text and headings only. Numerals and words in chapter titles, captions, labels, diagrams, charts, graphs, sidebars, and extra features are not included.

BRAVE SETTLERS IN A STRANGE LAND

by Donna Foley

illustrated by Ron Mahoney

PEARSON

Scott
Foresman

Editorial Offices: Glenview, Illinois • Parsippany, New Jersey • New York, New York
Sales Offices: Needham, Massachusetts • Duluth, Georgia • Glenview, Illinois
Coppell, Texas • Ontario, California • Mesa, Arizona

Glossary

attention *n.* careful thinking, looking, or listening.

complained *v.* to have said that you were unhappy, annoyed, or upset about something.

drifting *v.* carrying or being carried along by currents of air or water.

giggle *n.* a silly or uncontrolled laugh.

glaring *adj.* staring angrily.

looping *v.* forming a line, path, or motion shaped so that it crosses itself.

struggled *v.* tried hard; worked hard against difficulties.

swooping *v.* coming down fast on something, as a hawk does when it attacks.

Every effort has been made to secure permission and provide appropriate credit for photographic material. The publisher deeply regrets any omission and pledges to correct errors called to its attention in subsequent editions.

Unless otherwise acknowledged, all photographs are the property of Scott Foresman, a division of Pearson Education.

Photo locators denoted as follows: Top (T), Center (C), Bottom (B), Left (L), Right (R), Background (Bkgd)

Illustrations by Ron Mahoney

10 (C) S. Rubin/The Image Works, Inc.; (BL) S. Rubin/The Image Works, Inc.; 12 Stephen Chernin, Stringer/AP/Wide World Photos; 13 Michael Newman/PhotoEdit; 14 (CL) Spencer Platt/Newsmakers/Getty Images, (BL) Jeff Zelevansky/AP/Wide World Photos, (BR) DK Images

ISBN: 0-328-13368-X

Copyright © Pearson Education, Inc.

All Rights Reserved. Printed in the United States of America. This publication is protected by Copyright, and permission should be obtained from the publisher prior to any prohibited reproduction, storage in a retrieval system, or transmission in any form by any means, electronic, mechanical, photocopying, recording, or likewise. For information regarding permission(s), write to: Permissions Department, Scott Foresman, 1900 East Lake Avenue, Glenview, Illinois 60025.

2 3 4 5 6 7 8 9 10 V0G1 14 13 12 11 10 09 08 07 06 05

"Do you have any more stories about what it was like for her to be an immigrant?" Tommy asked.

"I sure do," said Grandpa. "She always said it was the hardest thing she ever did, and the best thing. Let's start our search by looking for the records of her ship!"

So Lisa, Tommy, and Grandpa spent a happy afternoon in the History Center. They learned about Grandpa's grandmother and the lives of the other brave immigrants who made homes for themselves in a strange new land.

15

As Tommy, Lisa, and Grandpa stood on the ferry, a voice called out over the loudspeaker. "Welcome to New York Harbor's Ellis Island. Ellis Island was the port of entry for millions of immigrants to America in the late 1800s and early 1900s."

Grandpa had told Tommy and Lisa stories about his grandmother, who came to Ellis Island from Europe. Now they were going to visit the island with him!

The park ranger guided the tour group into a new area. "This is the American Family Immigration History Center," he said. "Here, you can search for your ancestors' records. You can also listen to recordings made by immigrants who entered at Ellis Island. You can even research your family tree if you'd like!"

Lisa turned to Grandpa. "Can we search for Great-Great-Grandmother's records?" she asked.

"That's a wonderful idea!" said Grandpa.

Ellis Island's American Family Immigration History Center has many family records.

Birds were **swooping** and **drifting** through the air above the harbor. Their **glaring** eyes watched the ferry as it passed by. Tommy and Lisa stood by the ferry railing and listened as Grandpa spoke.

"When I was a child my grandmother told me many stories about coming to America," Grandpa said. "She told me about all of the different people who immigrated. They came from many different backgrounds. It was hard for them to leave their homes and come to a strange new land. But they came! They worked hard to make lives in America.

Lisa was thinking about today's immigrants to America. "Where do immigrants enter America today, now that Ellis Island is closed?" she asked the park ranger.

"California is the new Ellis Island," he answered. "It receives most of our country's new immigrants. They come from mainland Asia, the Philippines, Mexico, and Central America. They come by ship, by airplane, and by car."

Today most immigrants enter the United States through the state of California.

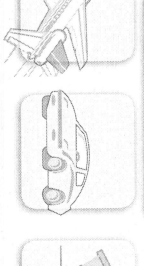

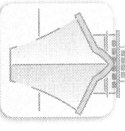

"Most people in the United States have family roots in other parts of the world," Grandpa said. "That's why America has been called a 'melting pot.'

"These days," he added, "immigrants aren't expected to give up their cultures to fit into society as was expected earlier. People are more respectful of immigrants' different traditions. But when my grandmother came to America, she had a hard time. Immigrants faced a lot of prejudice because they were different. They **struggled** to fit in. Can you imagine what it was like?"

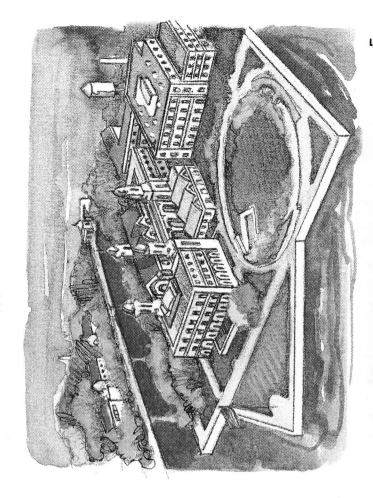

The park ranger led the tour group into another room. "Now we're in the Great Hall, or registry room," he said. "This is where immigrants waited to be examined. All immigrants had to pass a medical exam. They also needed to show documents in order to enter the United States."

"My grandmother told me about her examination," Grandpa told Tommy and Lisa. "She said that the immigrants were frightened. They were afraid they wouldn't be allowed to enter the United States. Luckily, all went well for her. She wasn't sick, and she had the right papers."

Immigrants were examined in the Great Hall at Ellis Island in New York.

"Grandpa, your head is in the clouds," Lisa said with a **giggle**. "Please pay **attention**. It's time to leave the ferry!"

Tommy, Lisa, and Grandpa joined the **looping** line of people. When they reached the bottom of the ferry ramp, Grandpa led them over to a park ranger who was about to start a tour.

"Hello, everyone, and welcome to Ellis Island," said the park ranger. "We start our tour today at the American Immigrant Wall of Honor.

"They sure did," said Grandpa. "The first Americans were actually the Native Americans. They settled in North America thousands of years before anyone else. Today, people are still coming to America."

"I wonder what it would be like to pick up and leave your home," Lisa said.

"Many immigrants had to work at jobs they'd never worked at before," said Grandpa. "They had to learn to live in new ways. But thanks to all of the brave immigrants who came to America, we have a country rich in different cultures and traditions!"

"This wall honors everyone who has immigrated to America through Ellis Island. It also honors people who immigrated through ports in Boston, Philadelphia, Baltimore, San Francisco, Miami, and New Orleans."

The park ranger gave them a moment to think about all of America's immigrants. "Now, let's move on to the main building," he said.

Tommy and Lisa looked at more photographs of old immigrant neighborhoods and listened as the park ranger spoke. "The United States is constantly changing," he said. "By 2003 33.5 million U.S. residents had been born in a foreign country! Of those people, about fifty-three percent were from Latin America. Another twenty-five percent were from Asia. America has become a very diverse country!"

"Americans came from everywhere, didn't they, Grandpa?" Lisa asked.

Modern-day families immigrate to the United States.

Inside the main building, Tommy looked at the photographs of New York's old immigrant neighborhoods. "It looks so crowded," he said. "There were so many people!"

"Yes," Grandpa replied, "people came from all over the world. My grandmother had neighbors from Russia, Germany, and Ireland. She couldn't talk to most of her neighbors because she didn't speak their languages. For a long time, she couldn't speak English either.

"She never **complained**, but I think she must have been lonely. She must have felt very different."

The park ranger continued speaking. "From 1880 to 1930, twenty-seven million people entered the United States. About twelve million of them came through Ellis Island. Most were from Europe and Canada.

"Immigration slowed down between 1930 and 1965. During those years, many immigrants came from Germany, Canada, Mexico, Britain, Italy, and Latin America. Today, many immigrants to the United States come from Asia and Mexico."

The Ellis Island Immigration Museum

From 1880 to 1930 about twelve million immigrants entered the United States through Ellis Island. Most were from Europe and Canada.

From 1930 to 1965 fewer immigrants came. Most were from Germany, Canada, Mexico, Britain, Italy, and Latin America. Today many come from Asia and Mexico.

Earth Science

Science

Science

Getting the Lay of the Land

Genre	Comprehension Skills and Strategy	Text Features
Expository nonfiction	• Compare and Contrast • Fact and Opinion • Ask Questions	• Maps • Diagram • Chart • Glossary

Scott Foresman Reading Street 3.4.2

PEARSON

Scott
Foresman

ISBN 0-328-13371-X

9 780328 133710

90000

Vocabulary

average

depth

desert

outrun

peak

tides

waterfalls

Word count: 997

Note: The total word count includes words in the running text and headings only.
Numerals and words in chapter titles, captions, labels, diagrams, charts, graphs,
sidebars, and extra features are not included.

Reader Response

1. Compare and contrast the two methods of measuring ocean depth described on pages 6 and 7. Use a graphic organizer to organize your information.

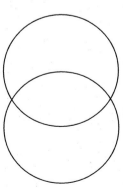

2. What question did you have while reading that was answered as you read further?

3. Find the compound words on pages 8 and 9. Write them in sentences of your own.

4. How does the Mohs Scale help you understand how scientists measure the hardness of different minerals?

Getting the Lay of the Land

by Patricia West

PEARSON

Scott Foresman

Editorial Offices: Glenview, Illinois • Parsippany, New Jersey • New York, New York
Sales Offices: Needham, Massachusetts • Duluth, Georgia • Glenview, Illinois
Coppell, Texas • Ontario, California • Mesa, Arizona

Glossary

average *n.* The quantity found by dividing the sum of all the quantities by the number of quantities.

depth *n.* the distance from the top to the bottom.

deserts *n.* dry, often sandy, regions without much water.

outrun *v.* to run faster than someone or something.

peak *n.* the pointed top of a mountain or hill.

tides *n.* the rising and falling of the ocean about every twelve hours. This rising and falling is caused by the gravitational pull of the Moon and the Sun.

waterfalls *n.* streams of water that fall from a high place.

Every effort has been made to secure permission and provide appropriate credit for photographic material. The publisher deeply regrets any omission and pledges to correct errors called to its attention in subsequent editions.

Unless otherwise acknowledged, all photographs are the property of Scott Foresman, a division of Pearson Education.

Photo locators denoted as follows: Top (T), Center (C), Bottom (B), Left (L), Right (R), Background (Bkgd)

Opener: Galen Rowell/Corbis; 1 Getty Images; 3 Galen Rowell/ Corbis; 4 Panoramic Images; 6 Digital Vision, (BL) Kindra Clineff/Index Stock Imagery; 7 (CL) Peter Hvizdak/The Image Works, Inc., (B) European Space Agency/Photo Researchers, Inc.; 8 (B) @Royalty-Free/Corbis, (BR) Robert Holm & Susan Van Etten/ PhotoEdit; 9 (TL) Thinkstock, (T) Jason Hawkes/Corbis; 10 Spencer Platt/Getty Images; 12 Colin Keates/DK Images; 13 (TL) Digital Vision, @DK Images; 14 (CR) Peter Hvizdak/ The Image Works, Inc., (B) Charles N. Corfield, (T) Cindy Charles/PhotoEdit

ISBN: 0-328-13371-X

Measuring Marvels

People have invented amazing ways to measure things! Our instruments are very good at measuring. But Earth's landforms are always changing. The Himalayas are growing and changing. The depths of the oceans are increasing and decreasing. Because of that, some measurements will always be a little out-of-date.

Even so, our measuring instruments give us a snapshot of many of Earth's measurements as they are right now. They teach us about Earth and clear up mysteries. And scientists are coming up with newer and better measuring instruments all the time!

The Height of a Mountain

How do you measure a mountain? If mountains were shaped in straight lines, it would be easy. You could go to the top of a mountain and drop a string to the bottom. Then you could measure the string's length. But you can't do that because mountains have uneven shapes. Also, the ground under them isn't flat. That's because the Earth is curved.

Suddenly, measuring mountains looks like a difficult job! So how is it done? Keep reading to find out.

A scientist reads a seismograph in a California laboratory.

A fish-shaped sonar instrument can search for objects on the ocean floor.

A GPS station sits on rocks that face Mount Everest in the Himalayas.

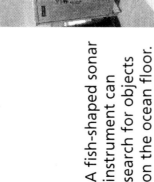

Mount Everest is a **peak** in the Himalayas. The Himalayas are a range of mountains on the continent of Asia.

A very long time ago the land that is now India began to push against the land that is now China. That caused the Himalayas to form. The height of the Himalayas is an **average** of 27,000 feet. And the mountain range is still growing!

Mount Everest was named for a British explorer, Sir George Everest. For years, people wondered how tall Mount Everest was.

This chalk is made of gypsum, a soft mineral that leaves a powdery streak.

The softest mineral in the world is talc. You can crush it easily in your hand! Because talc is so soft, it was given a 1 on the Mohs Scale.

Your fingernail has a hardness of about 2.5 on the Mohs Scale. That means it is harder than both talc and gypsum. A penny has a hardness of 3 on the Mohs Scale. That means it is harder than your fingernail. And diamond, which measures 10 on the scale, is hardest of all!

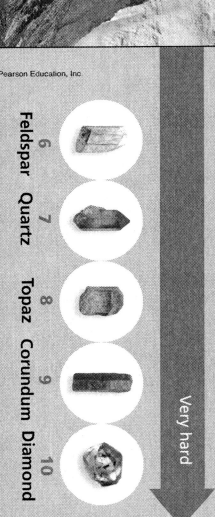

6 Feldspar 7 Quartz 8 Topaz 9 Corundum 10 Diamond

Very hard

In 1999 Mount Everest measured 29,035 feet high, the tallest mountain on Earth. How was that measurement made?

A satellite circling the Earth sent radio signals down to the Earth's surface. A radio receiver at the top of Mount Everest picked up one of the signals. When the signal was picked up, the computer in the receiver was able to figure out the exact height of the mountain!

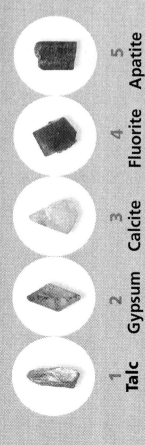

Mount Everest is Earth's tallest mountain.

Measuring Minerals

There are many natural things that you can measure other than mountains, oceans, and earthquakes. For example, you can measure minerals.

When scientists study a mineral, they measure its size, weight, and hardness. The Mohs Scale is used to measure a mineral's hardness. This scale uses certain minerals as examples of different hardnesses. You can then take other minerals and compare them to the ones on the scale.

Mohs Scale

Very soft

1	2	3	4	5
Talc	Gypsum	Calcite	Fluorite	Apatite

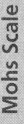

The Depth of an Ocean

In the past, it was not easy to measure the **depth** of the ocean. Sailors tied a heavy weight to the end of a rope. Then they let the rope down into the water.

The rope had knots in it. The knots were spaced every six feet. Sailors measured the depth of the water by counting the number of knots as they let the rope down into the water.

This method of measuring could take many hours. And it wasn't exact because the **tides** raised and lowered the water level!

Many years ago, sailors used knotted rope to measure ocean depth.

Locating an Earthquake

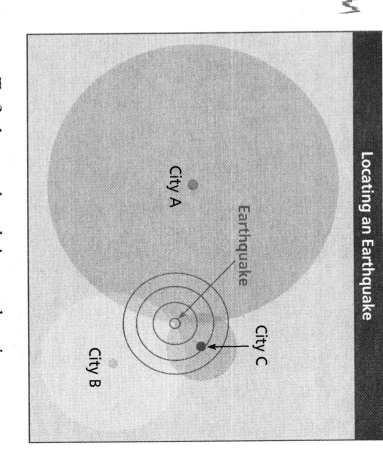

To find an earthquake's exact location, scientists measure the earthquake's distance from three cities. A seismograph in City A shows that an earthquake happened 200 miles away. A seismograph in City B shows that the same earthquake happened 100 miles away. A seismograph in City C shows that the same earthquake happened 50 miles away.

Scientists draw a circle 200 miles out from City A, 100 miles out from City B, and 50 miles out from City C. The spot where all three circles touch is the earthquake's exact location!

Today, scientists use sonar, or sound waves, to measure ocean depth. The sonar sends a "ping" sound to the bottom of the ocean. The ping sound hits the ocean bottom and bounces back to the ship. A timer keeps track of how long it takes the sound to travel down and back. Sound travels about 5,000 feet per second in water. Knowing that, and using the timer, scientists can tell how far the sound traveled to reach the ocean bottom. That tells them how deep the ocean is.

A research ship uses sonar to measure the depth of the ocean.

The colors on this map show the different depths of Earth's oceans.

Earthquake!

It's important to measure distances when earthquakes happen. Scientists can pinpoint an earthquake's location by using seismographs, instruments that measure earthquake waves.

An earthquake makes two kinds of waves that travel through the ground. One kind of wave travels faster than the other. By measuring the time it has taken the waves to travel, the seismograph can tell how far away an earthquake happened.

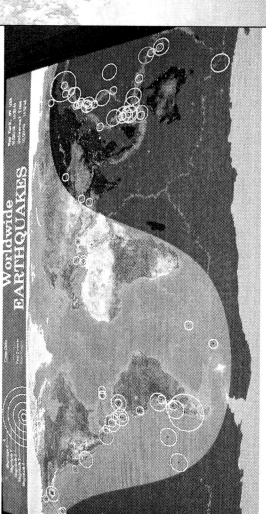

An earthquake screen shows the shaking of Earth's ground.

Lost!

Another modern invention is the Global Positioning System, or GPS. GPS helps people keep track of where they are.

GPS picks up different satellite signals. The system pinpoints the exact place on Earth where those signals meet. That place, or position, is the location of the GPS user.

People who use GPS never have to worry about finding their way out of **deserts**. There's also no need to **outrun** the setting sun. GPS works just fine in the dark!

A hiker uses the GPS method to track his location.

An odometer measures the number of miles traveled.

Are We There Yet!

The odometer in a car measures the distance the car has traveled. Suppose that you're driving with your family to see some **waterfalls.** You know that the trip is one hundred miles long. But how do you know how many miles you have driven at each point along the way? The car's odometer can give you the answer!

The odometer is attached to a car's axle. It keeps track of how many times the car wheels rotate, or turn, on the axle. That's how the odometer shows how far a car has traveled.

Earth Science

Science

Science

Fun with Science!

by Kelly Kong

Genre	Comprehension Skills and Strategy	Text Features
Expository nonfiction	• Generalize • Draw Conclusions • Prior Knowledge	• Captions • Labels • Heads • Glossary

Scott Foresman Reading Street 3.4.3

PEARSON

Scott Foresman

ISBN 0-328-13374-4

9 780328 133741

90000

Vocabulary

attic

board

chores

customers

label

spare

stamps

Word count: 801

Note: The total word count includes words in the running text and headings only. Numerals and words in chapter titles, captions, labels, diagrams, charts, graphs, sidebars, and extra features are not included.

Reader Response

1. Write a general statement about binoculars and telescopes.

2. Before you read this book, what did you know about archaeologists? What do you know about archaeologists now? What would you still like to learn about archaeologists? Use a graphic organizer like the one below to show your thoughts.

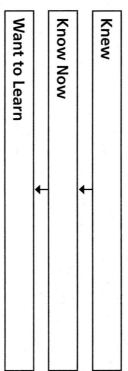

Knew

Know Now

Want to Learn

3. There are three vocabulary words in this book that are plural words. Which ones are they? Use them in sentences of your own.

4. Go back to the part of the book that talks about birds. According to the book, how long can a hummingbird be? How large can an eagle's wingspan be?

Fun with Science!

by Kelly Kong

PEARSON

Scott Foresman

Editorial Offices: Glenview, Illinois • Parsippany, New Jersey • New York, New York
Sales Offices: Needham, Massachusetts • Duluth, Georgia • Glenview, Illinois
Coppell, Texas • Ontario, California • Mesa, Arizona

Glossary

attic *n.* the space in a house just below the roof and above the other rooms.

board *n.* a broad, thin piece of wood for use in building.

chores *n.* small tasks or easy jobs that you have to do regularly.

customers *n.* people who buy goods or services.

labeled *v.* to put or write a label on something.

spare *adj.* extra.

stamps *n.* small pieces of paper with glue on the back; postage stamps.

Every effort has been made to secure permission and provide appropriate credit for photographic material. The publisher deeply regrets any omission and pledges to correct errors called to its attention in subsequent editions.

Unless otherwise acknowledged, all photographs are the property of Scott Foresman, a division of Pearson Education.

Photo locators denoted as follows: Top (T), Center (C), Bottom (B), Left (L), Right (R), Background (Bkgd)

Opener: Angus Beare/DK Images, (C) Arthur Morris/Corbis, (B) Gary Ombler/DK Images; 1 Getty Images; 3 (C) Tony Freeman/PhotoEdit, (CR) Spencer Grant/PhotoEdit, (BR) Momatiuk Eastcott/The Image Works, Inc., (BL) Getty Images, ©Comstock Inc.; 4 (TR) Spencer Grant/PhotoEdit, (CL) ©Kenneth Garret/NGS Image Collection, (BR) Tony Freeman/PhotoEdit; 5 Digital Stock, (R) ©Royalty-Free/Corbis; (BR) Tom Vezo/Peter Arnold, Inc., (BR) Larry West/Getty Images, (T) Arthur Morris/Corbis; 8 ©Royalty-Free Corbis; 9 (BL) Cathy Melloan/PhotoEdit, (CR) Bill Aron/PhotoEdit; 10 (C) Getty Images, (B) ©Royalty-Free/Corbis; 11 David Young-Wolff/PhotoEdit; 12 (B) ©Royalty-Free/ Corbis, (L) Getty Images; 13 Getty Images, 14 (TL) Getty Images, (B) Kevin Fleming/ Corbis; 15 Jeff Greenberg/Index Stock Imagery

As you have learned, many hobbies are related to science. And who knows? The science hobby that you start today could become your job in the future.

Science is a part of our daily lives. Turn your interests into hobbies to learn and have fun!

Hobbies are fun and can teach you a lot about science.

15

It's the weekend and you have finished your **chores.** What will you do with your free time? Maybe you will play a game or read a book. There are many ways to spend your **spare** time!

You probably have many hobbies. Some may take you outside. Others may involve friends or adults. One of your hobbies could even become your job one day! Did you know that many hobbies are related to science?

Fun with Hobbies

There are many other popular science hobbies out there. If you love animals, you can help take care of them. What you learn about animals now may help you become a veterinarian in the future! A veterinarian is a doctor who takes care of animals.

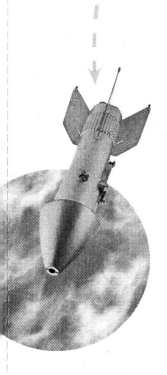

Caring for animals can be an interesting hobby!

Zoology?

For example, do you enjoy taking care of animals? Scientists who study animals are called zoologists.

Archeology?

Do you like digging around in search of old objects? Archeologists are people who use clues found in today's world to study history and past cultures.

Astronomy?

Maybe you like watching the stars? An astronomer studies outer space.

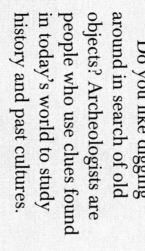

Each of these hobbies is connected to science. Read on to find out more about the connections between hobbies and science!

Space has been called the final frontier. That is because it contains many mysteries and was difficult to study in the past.

Telescopes are tools that make observing space and the stars easier. Telescopes are made up of a set of lenses, mirrors, or both. They are used to make objects in the sky appear closer. You may use a small telescope when you stargaze.

Astronomers use huge, powerful telescopes to study planets and stars that are trillions of miles away. Astronomers have learned many things by watching the night sky.

Saturn

A hummingbird is a tiny bird.

Learning from Animals

Have you ever spotted a bluebird flying across the sky? Have you ever seen a red cardinal sitting on a tree branch? Birds are incredible creatures. They come in many different shapes, sizes, and colors.

Birds can be tiny. Some hummingbirds are only two inches long! Other birds are much larger. Eagles have wingspans of almost eight feet! Birds can be very different from each other. A simple but powerful tool makes it easy to spot birds' differences.

Watching the Night Sky

Do you enjoy gazing up at a dark sky filled with twinkling stars? Stargazing is another popular hobby that relates to science. People have watched the stars in the night sky for thousands of years.

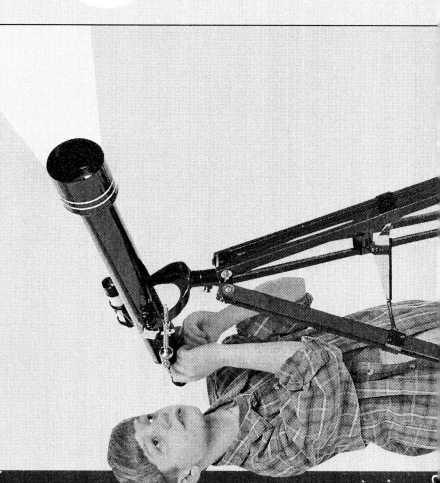

The simple but powerful tool is a set of binoculars! Binoculars make faraway objects appear closer. With binoculars you can watch birds find food, eat, or care for their young.

Birds are often fearful of people. If you are farther away, it is less likely birds can hear or smell you. That means you are more likely to see the birds behave normally.

Watching birds and other animals is important. It helps zoologists understand more about their life cycles. By learning about animals' habits, zoologists can help them survive in their environments.

Use binoculars to watch birds without disturbing them.

Before you start digging holes in search of lost treasures, however, it is important that you ask for permission from an adult. When you find something that is interesting, ask an adult to help you identify it.

Hidden treasures may be buried in your own backyard.

These statues are treasures from the past!

Scarlet tanager

Eastern bluebird

Flicker

Archeology

Workers in China were digging a well to provide water for local people. As one worker dug, his shovel hit a hard object. He had hit a buried statue. Archeologists heard about the statue and visited the workers. When the archeologists dug deeper, they found a group of statues that were more than two thousand years old! Nobody had known that the statues existed. Archeologists researched the past to learn more about the treasured statues.

Digging Up the Past

Have you ever found old items in an attic? People sometimes like to save old items, such as **stamps** or an oil painting on an old **board**. Then they may sell them to **customers** at a yard sale.

Old and ancient items are found every day in many different places. When an ancient item is found, it often tells something about past peoples, cultures, and places.

It is fun to find old treasures from the past. Sometimes old items are **labeled.** Other times they are not. When items are not labeled and you do not know what they are, you can research the past to learn more about them!

You can learn about the past by talking to your family and neighbors, searching your attic, or going to the library and reading old newspapers.

Talk to a neighbor or visit your library for more information about the past.

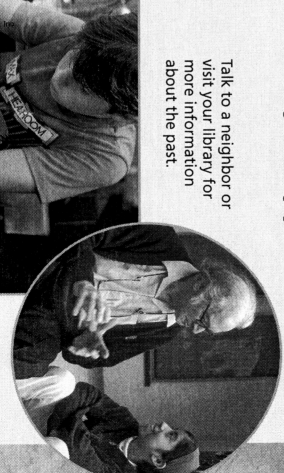

Biography

Social Studies

Social Studies

Women Who Made a Difference

by Megan Litwin

Illustrated by Alohan Inacay

Genre	Comprehension Skills and Strategy	Text Features
Biography	• Fact and Opinion • Main Idea and Details • Monitor and Fix Up	• Headings • Captions • Glossary

Scott Foresman Reading Street 3.4.4

PEARSON

Scott Foresman

ISBN 0-328-13377-9

9 780328 133772

90000

Vocabulary

celebrate

continued

current

drowned

medal

stirred

strokes

Word count: 830

Note: The total word count includes words in the running text and headings only. Numerals and words in chapter titles, captions, labels, diagrams, charts, graphs, sidebars, and extra features are not included.

Reader Response

1. Reread page 7. Find one example of a fact and one of an opinion. Tell why you would identify them that way.

2. Write a statement about each woman in this book telling why she was famous. Use a word web like this one to help you organize details about their accomplishments. Make one word web for each woman.

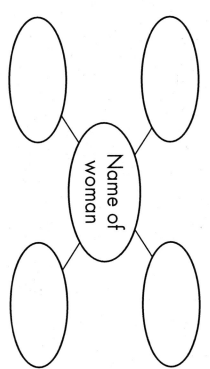

Name of woman

3. The words *current* and *strokes* have meanings other than the ones listed in the glossary. Use a dictionary to find another meaning for each word. Use each word in a sentence to show this other meaning.

4. Which of the three women do you think was the most daring? Why?

Women Who Made a Difference

by Megan Litwin

illustrated by Aleksey Ivanov

Editorial Offices: Glenview, Illinois • Parsippany, New Jersey • New York, New York
Sales Offices: Needham, Massachusetts • Duluth, Georgia • Glenview, Illinois
Coppell, Texas • Ontario, California • Mesa, Arizona

Glossary

celebrate *v.* to honor or praise.

continued *v.* went on in some action; kept on.

current *adj.* belonging to the present; in progress.

drowned *v.* died by suffocation in water.

medal *n.* a small piece of metal, usually with a special design, given as an award for some outstanding act.

stirred *v.* awakened or brought to the surface (as in an emotion).

strokes *n.* in tennis, golf, or other ball sports, the motion of striking or hitting the ball.

Many years ago, women could not vote, go to college, or hold a well-paying job. Women had to fight against tremendous odds to win those rights. Today, women can go to college, vote, and work at any job they please. Let's look at three remarkable women who made a difference in U.S. history: Babe Didrikson Zaharias, Amelia Earhart, and Eleanor Roosevelt.

Many years ago, women could not go to college. Today, women can achieve almost anything they want.

Babe Didrikson Zaharias

Babe Didrikson Zaharias was born in Texas in 1911. Her real name was Mildred Ella Didrikson, but the neighborhood kids called her "Babe" because she could hit a baseball as well as Babe Ruth.

Babe loved baseball. She didn't care that people told her it was a boy's game. She knew she was just as strong as any boy.

Even as a child, Babe Didrikson Zaharias was a strong batter and a terrific athlete.

Babe Didrikson Zaharias, Amelia Earhart, and Eleanor Roosevelt were three great women in U.S. history. They worked hard to gain respect for all women. Their determination and bravery led them to do things no one had done before. Every one of us can **celebrate** their successes. Each of us can learn from their courage and spirit.

Amelia Earhart

Eleanor Roosevelt

Babe Didrikson Zaharias

13

It didn't take Babe long to prove she was good at other sports too. In high school, Babe was a star on the basketball team. In 1930, Babe was named an All-American. That meant she was one of the best players in the country.

Babe wanted to succeed at other sports as well. She loved to run the hurdles because it reminded her of running and jumping over the hedges when she was a child. Babe was so good at track-and-field events that the newspapers called her "Texas Tornado." She set records at track meets.

Babe played basketball in high school.

Eleanor traveled across the country and **stirred** hope in the hearts of millions of people. Her motto was "Tomorrow is now." Eleanor helped the poor, and she spoke out for the rights of women and other minorities. She told people, "Do what you feel in your heart to be right."

Even after her husband's death, Eleanor **continued** her work. She fought for human rights and worked for peace. When she died on November 7, 1962, she was one of the most important and beloved women of her time.

Eleanor Roosevelt gave many speeches across the country.

In 1932, Babe went to the Olympic Games in Los Angeles. She set a world record in the javelin throw. A javelin is a type of spear. She won a gold **medal.** Next, Babe took up golfing. Her golf **strokes** were so strong that she became a champion at that too. In 1950, she was named the Outstanding Woman Athlete of the Half-Century. She died of cancer at a young age, but her memory and courage will live forever.

Babe won an Olympic Gold Medal in the javelin throw.

Then, in 1921, Franklin was stricken with polio. Eleanor became his nurse, but she was much more than that. She began to travel to political meetings for her husband. She saw many injustices and spoke out against them.

Franklin was elected President of the United States in 1932. Eleanor became First Lady. She began to study **current** events. The 1930s was the time of the Great Depression in the United States. Many people had no work or money for food.

When Franklin could no longer walk, Eleanor began to travel for him.

11

Amelia Earhart

Amelia Earhart was a famous airplane pilot. But she was even more famous for her sense of adventure. She would not take "no" for an answer. She was born on July 24, 1897, in Kansas. Like Babe, Amelia was a tomboy.

Most people didn't think that women should fly planes. Amelia decided to learn to fly anyway. She worked many jobs to pay for her flying lessons. In 1922, her family helped her buy her first plane. Amelia received her pilot's license in 1923.

Amelia's first plane, *Canary*, was canary yellow.

Eleanor Roosevelt

Eleanor Roosevelt was born on October 11, 1884, in New York City. She grew up in a wealthy family, but money didn't cure her loneliness. It wasn't until Eleanor went to boarding school that she began to see how helping others could make her happy. That was a lesson Eleanor would try to teach others all her life. In 1905, Eleanor married Franklin D. Roosevelt.

As a child, Eleanor learned that she loved helping others.

One day in 1928, Amelia was asked to take part in a dangerous flight. A male pilot and his navigator were flying a plane called *Friendship* across the Atlantic Ocean. Amelia joined them. She became the first woman to fly across the Atlantic.

In 1932, she became even more famous when she flew a plane across the Atlantic by herself. "Can she bake a cake?" the French newspapers asked. Amelia knew she could do that and so much more.

Crowds cheered Amelia's spirit and bravery.

Amelia wanted to fly along the equator and circle the entire Earth. It was very risky. No woman had ever done that before! But Amelia had spirit.

Amelia finished two-thirds of the flight. Then, on July 3, 1937, something went wrong. Amelia and her plane disappeared. No one knows for sure what happened. Maybe her plane ran out of fuel, or maybe she **drowned**. We do know that Amelia Earhart proved that women can do daring things.

Planes searched for Amelia, but she and her plane have never been found.

The Lost Dog

by Thea Feldman

Genre	Comprehension Skills and Strategy	
Realistic fiction	• Plot and Theme • Sequence • Graphic Organizers	

Scott Foresman Reading Street 3.4.5

PEARSON

Scott
Foresman

ISBN 0-328-13380-9

9 780328 133802

90000

Reader Response

1. What happened at the beginning of the story? What happened in the middle? What happened at the end?

2. Think about the part of the story with the rabbit in it. Use a chart like the one below to show what happened and why.

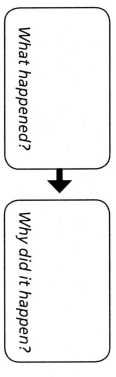

   What happened? → *Why did it happen?*

3. Write a short paragraph describing a mountain setting. Use the words you find in this book and add others you know.

4. Do you have a dog or another kind of pet? If not, what kind of pet would you like to have? What activities can a child and a pet do together?

Vocabulary

clutched

echoed

gully

reeds

scrambled

valley

Word count: 908

Note: The total word count includes words in the running text and headings only. Numerals and words in chapter titles, captions, labels, diagrams, charts, graphs, sidebars, and extra features are not included.

The Lost Dog

by Thea Feldman
illustrated by Tom LaBaff

PEARSON
Scott Foresman

Editorial Offices: Glenview, Illinois • Parsippany, New Jersey • New York, New York
Sales Offices: Needham, Massachusetts • Duluth, Georgia • Glenview, Illinois
Coppell, Texas • Ontario, California • Mesa, Arizona

Animal Instincts

There have been many cases of dogs traveling long distances to get back to their owners. They use their instincts, or behaviors they are born with. Instincts do not need to be taught.

Hounds, like beagles, love to chase other animals, such as rabbits. Following a scent trail is a natural instinct for hounds.

All dogs use their noses to make sense of the world around them. Do you know any dogs? Maybe you have a dog of your own. Watch a dog for an hour. Does the dog use its sense of smell more than its other senses? Try to find out!

Beagles using their noses to investigate

16

Illustrations by Tom LaBaff

Photograph 16 Corbis

ISBN: 0-328-13380-9

Copyright © Pearson Education, Inc.

All Rights Reserved. Printed in the United States of America. This publication is protected by Copyright, and permission should be obtained from the publisher prior to any prohibited reproduction, storage in a retrieval system, or transmission in any form by any means, electronic, mechanical, photocopying, recording, or likewise. For information regarding permission(s), write to: Permissions Department, Scott Foresman, 1900 East Lake Avenue, Glenview, Illinois 60025.

2 3 4 5 6 7 8 9 10 V0G1 14 13 12 11 10 09 08 07 06 05

Another long week went by. Sam woke up on Saturday morning to the sound of barking. The bark sounded just like Buddy's! Sam ran to his front door and pulled it open. He could not believe his eyes! There was Buddy, sitting on the welcome mat. He was wagging his tail harder than ever!

Sam was so surprised! "Good boy! You followed the scent trail!" he cried happily. Sam knelt down, and Buddy scrambled into his arms. Sam clutched his dog tightly. "Welcome home, Buddy! Welcome home!"

15

"I can't believe the weekend is over already," Sam said. "Thanks for inviting Buddy and me up to your cabin. We had a great time!"

"I did too. I can't believe my parents are packing the car to go home already," said Alan. "It was fun having you here. And Buddy never ran out of things to sniff!"

Buddy yipped and went back to sniffing the ground.

Sam stayed hopeful, but he was sad. He didn't want to play with his friends. He didn't even want pizza, his favorite food. All he wanted was Buddy.

Sam's mother offered to get him another dog, but Sam wasn't interested. He read in his library book that beagles are born with the instinct to hunt. He learned that beagles are experts at finding and following a scent. Sam knew that leaving that scent trail had been a wise thing to do. He was not ready to give up on Buddy.

Suddenly, the reeds by the bank of the mountain stream made a whooshing sound. A rabbit bounded out and scampered right in front of the boys!

"Wow!" Alan exclaimed. "That rabbit ran by so fast! I almost missed it!"

"It must have been taking a drink in that gully next to the stream," Sam said. "We probably startled it."

Sam's class spent time in the school library that week, and Sam chose a book about beagles to take home. He wanted to learn everything he could about beagles and their instincts.

There was no news about Buddy that week. On the weekend, Sam and his mom traveled to the mountain cabins. Mr. Hall and Alan went along too. But they didn't find Buddy.

Buddy had seen the rabbit too. His yips changed to a loud bark. The rabbit disappeared into the tall grass, and Buddy ran after it. His tail wagged excitedly.

"Wait, boy! Buddy, come back!" Sam shouted. But the dog didn't return. The boys could not see him anywhere. Sam ran after Buddy, and Alan headed back to the cabin to get his dad.

Sam's mom gave him a big hug when he got home. After he told her about Buddy, she hugged him again.

"If we don't hear anything by the weekend, we'll go and look for him again," Mom promised.

The days and nights were long for Sam. He missed taking his dog for walks and playing with him after school. He missed having Buddy curled up at his feet while he did his homework. Most of all, he missed the yipping sounds Buddy made in his sleep at night.

"Buddy!" Sam called over and over. "Buddy! Come back, boy! It's time to go home!" But the only thing Sam heard was his own voice as it echoed off the mountain.

Alan and Mr. Hall made their way through the tall grass. They caught up with Sam at the edge of the mountain forest.

On the way home Sam threw a few small pieces of his clothing out the car window. His idea was that Buddy would find them and pick up his scent. Then his dog could follow the scent home.

Sam watched for Buddy all the way down the mountain road. But he didn't see any dogs at all.

11

"Sam, it looks as though Buddy is far ahead of us," said Mr. Hall.

"Well, how do we get through this underbrush?" Sam asked. "I'm sure that Buddy is somewhere in the forest!"

"The brush is too thick, Sam," said Mr. Hall gently. "We'd have to be Buddy's size to move around safely in there."

"So what do we do?" Sam asked. He was trying not to panic.

"We can wait here awhile and see if Buddy comes back," said Mr. Hall.

"I can't leave Buddy up here alone!" Sam said. He couldn't face the thought of leaving his best friend behind.

"Here's what we'll do," said Mr. Hall. "We'll post a sign about Buddy at the cabin rental office. Buddy has tags on his collar with his name and your phone number. I'm sure someone will find him in a day or two and give you a call."

Sam, Alan, and Mr. Hall waited for an hour. They called Buddy's name until their voices were hoarse. But the dog did not come back.

"Why would Buddy run off like that?" Alan wondered aloud as they walked back through the tall grass toward the cabin.

"Well," replied Mr. Hall, "Buddy is a beagle. He's doing what beagles do. They like to chase things."

"But why didn't he come back?" Sam pleaded. "Something must have happened to him!"

"Sam, we don't know that. Buddy is probably a little turned around. He hasn't been up in the mountain forest before."

"That's right," Sam said.

"I'm sorry, Sam, but when we get back to the cabin, it will be time to head home. We have a long drive back to the valley."

Dressed for School Success

by Linda Lott

Social Studies

Suggested levels for Guided Reading, DRA,™ Lexile,® and Reading Recovery™ are provided in the Pearson Scott Foresman Leveling Guide.

Genre	Comprehension Skills and Strategy	Text Features
Expository nonfiction	• Compare and Contrast • Main Idea • Predict	• Captions • Labels • Heads • Glossary

Scott Foresman Reading Street 3.5.1

ISBN 0-328-13383-3

9 780328 133833

90000

PEARSON

Scott Foresman

Vocabulary

cotton

festival

graceful

handkerchief

pace

pale

rhythm

snug

Word count: 731

Note: The total word count includes words in the running text and headings only. Numerals and words in chapter titles, captions, labels, diagrams, charts, graphs, sidebars, and extra features are not included.

Reader Response

1. Compare and contrast the school clothes worn to "dame schools" with your own school clothes.

2. Predict the kind of clothing schoolchildren might be wearing one hundred years from now.

3. Make a web like the one below. Around it, write words from the book that relate to school clothes.

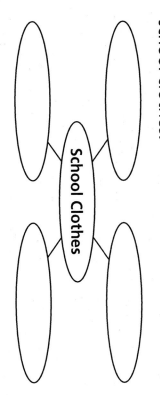

School Clothes

4. Go back into the selection. Which kind of school clothes did you find most interesting? Tell why.

Dressed for School Success

by Linda Lott

PEARSON
Scott
Foresman

Editorial Offices: Glenview, Illinois • Parsippany, New Jersey • New York, New York
Sales Offices: Needham, Massachusetts • Duluth, Georgia • Glenview, Illinois
Coppell, Texas • Ontario, California • Mesa, Arizona

Glossary

cotton *adj.* cloth made from soft, white fibers that grow in fluffy bunches on the cotton plant.

festival *n.* a program of entertainment, often held annually.

graceful *adj.* beautiful in form or movement.

handkerchief *n.* a soft, usually square piece of cloth used for wiping your nose, face, or hands.

pace *n.* a step.

pale *adj.* not bright.

rhythm *n.* the natural strong beat that some music or poetry has.

snug *adj.* fitting your body closely.

ISBN: 0-328-13383-3

Copyright © Pearson Education, Inc.

All Rights Reserved. Printed in the United States of America. This publication is protected by Copyright, and permission should be obtained from the publisher prior to any prohibited reproduction, storage in a retrieval system, or transmission in any form by any means, electronic, mechanical, photocopying, recording, or likewise. For information regarding permission(s), write to: Permissions Department, Scott Foresman, 1900 East Lake Avenue, Glenview, Illinois 60025.

2 3 4 5 6 7 8 9 10 V0G1 14 13 12 11 10 09 08 07 06 05

Do you wear a school uniform?

Students in Africa wear clothes that keep them cool. They live far away from the United States. But their clothes are similar to what American children wear during the hot summer.

School clothes have changed over time. What do you think students will wear to school one hundred years from today?

15

What did you wear to school today? Maybe you wore a uniform. If the weather was warm, you may have worn shorts. Did your school have a play or a **festival?** If so, you may have worn a costume.

What if you were a student many years ago? The clothes you would have worn may have been very uncomfortable. School clothing has changed a lot over the years.

Are these students dressed the same as you?

Today's Choices

Today, schoolchildren all over the world wear uniforms or everyday clothes to school, just as you do.

Iranian girls dress for school in uniforms similar to those worn at private schools in the United States. Moslem girls may wear scarves over their heads, since that is a custom of their religion.

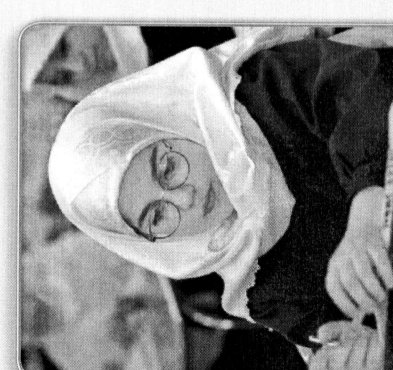

There are many different types of school uniforms.

Ancient Greece Dress

The ancient Greeks went to some of the earliest schools. Only wealthy boys went to school, though.

Greek students wore the same kinds of clothes as their parents. They wore pale cotton garments called chitons. A chiton was square-shaped. Chitons were very easy to make. They were also easy to put on.

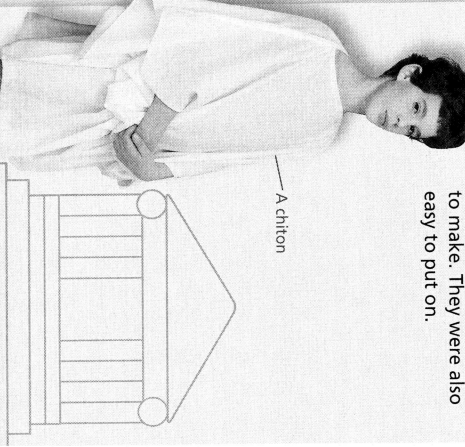

A chiton

Children who attended private schools wore uniforms. For boys, the uniform might have been dark pants and a white shirt. Girls often wore plaid skirts, or jumpers with white blouses.

At both public and private schools, saddle shoes were very popular with girls. Boys liked to wear loafers. Sneakers usually were worn only during physical education classes.

13

English School Outfits

During the Middle Ages, almost no one went to school. But the Age of the Renaissance followed. Learning became important again.

New schools were built. But they were mostly for wealthy boys. English boys wore tights under short pants, called breeches. They wore a doublet, or jacket, over a shirt. Some clothing was **snug** and uncomfortable.

English schoolboys wore many layers of clothing.

Changing School Dress

By the 1950s, many schools had strict dress codes. These were rules about what could be worn to school.

In most schools, girls wore skirts and blouses, or dresses. Ankle socks, knee socks, or tights covered their legs. They were not allowed to wear pants to school.

Boys wore shirts, neckties, and long pants. Many schools did not allow jeans. Hats were allowed. But boys had to show respect by taking their hats off when they entered the school building.

During the 1950s, boys were not allowed to wear jeans to school, and girls had to wear dresses or skirts.

Larger, city schools offered more classes. Health class, music class, and physical education were some of the new subjects.

Students learned about cleanliness in health class. They even had to bring a clean cotton **handkerchief** along. They learned about **rhythm**, reading music, and playing instruments in music class. Students changed into different clothing for physical education. They had to be able to move around and run at a fast **pace**.

Students wore different clothes during physical education.

"Dame School" Dress

Later, many European families settled in America. But they had to build schools for their children. Some children went to a "dame school." This meant that a woman teacher taught students in her home.

Students wore clothes made of **cotton,** linen, or wool. The girls wore petticoats, or slips, underneath their dresses. The boys dressed in short, buttoned breeches, with jackets or vests over their loose-fitting, long-sleeved shirts.

These children never had to worry about putting a shoe on the wrong foot. There was no such thing as right-footed shoes or left-footed shoes. Both shoes were the same!

Children learned reading and writing at the home of their teacher.

Not all families were pioneers. Many moved to cities. Immigrants came to cities too. City schools became quite crowded.

Girls in city schools wore long dresses that reached their shoes. Some boys wore short pants, called knickers, with stockings. Others wore long pants. Many boys wore jackets over their shirts.

A crowded city school

19

Pioneer Schoolchildren

Pioneer children could only attend school when they were not working on their families' farms.

Children of pioneer families did not own much clothing. Many children did not even wear shoes to school. Shoes were very expensive!

Boys wore shirts that buttoned in the front and pants. Some boys wore overalls. The girls wore long dresses, petticoats, and sunbonnets. Girls usually played quiet games at recess. It was hard to be a **graceful** runner in a long skirt with a petticoat underneath!

Farm children only attended school after the harvest, because they had to help with farm work.

Social Studies

What's in a Name?

by Sharon Franklin

Genre	Comprehension Skills and Strategy	Text Features
Expository nonfiction	• Fact and Opinion • Compare and Contrast • Text Structure	• Captions • Heads • Charts • Glossary

Scott Foresman Reading Street 3.5.2

PEARSON

Scott
Foresman

ISBN 0-328-13386-8

9 780328 133864

90000

Vocabulary

admire

custom

famous

mention

overnight

popular

public

twist

Word count: 1,151

Reader Response

1. Reread page 7, including the picture caption. Find one opinion, and explain how you know it is an opinion.

2. Review the naming customs on pages 8 and 9. Use a Venn diagram to compare and contrast the naming ceremonies.

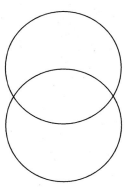

3. On page 14, the book says that people do not become famous overnight. Here, *overnight* is an adverb. Use *overnight* in a sentence so that it is an adjective.

4. If you were to add your given name to the chart on page 17, what information would you need? Using the library or the Internet, find out which country your name comes from and its meaning.

admire *v.* to look at with wonder, pleasure, and approval.

custom *n.* old or popular way of doing things.

famous *adj.* very well known; noted.

mention *v.* to tell or speak about something.

overnight *adv.* during the night.

popular *adj.* liked by most people.

public *adj.* of or for everyone; belonging to the people.

twist *n.* an unexpected variation.

What's in a Name?

by Sharon Franklin

Editorial Offices: Glenview, Illinois • Parsippany, New Jersey • New York, New York
Sales Offices: Needham, Massachusetts • Duluth, Georgia • Glenview, Illinois
Coppell, Texas • Ontario, California • Mesa, Arizona

Every effort has been made to secure permission and provide appropriate credit for photographic material. The publisher deeply regrets any omission and pledges to correct errors called to its attention in subsequent editions.

Unless otherwise acknowledged, all photographs are the property of Scott Foresman, a division of Pearson Education.

Photo locators denoted as follows: Top (T), Center (C), Bottom (B), Left (L), Right (R), Background (Bkgd)

Opener: Corbis, Comstock; 1 Comstock; 3 ©DK Images; 4 thinkstock; 5 Medio Images, Getty Images; 6 Getty Image; 7 Getty Images; 8 Getty Images; 9 Getty Images;10 Getty Images; 11 Getty Images; 12 Getty Images; 13 Getty Images; 14 Getty Images; 15 Getty Images; 17 John Foxx, Corbis, Image Source, Brand X Pictures; 18 Brand X Pictures; 19 Comstock

ISBN: 0-328-13386-8

A Final Word on Names

Our names are important to us and to others. It is important to remember to be respectful when meeting someone, especially if the name or culture of the person is new to you.

When you are introduced, listen carefully. Try to pronounce the name and ask if you are saying it correctly. If you are curious, you may ask how the person got his or her name. You may **mention** what you know about your own name as well.

Names are important. Without names, life would be very confusing. We identify ourselves with names. We name pets, towns, rivers, spaceships, and even stars. Plants and animals even have two names—a common name and a scientific name.

In this book you'll learn about names in different cultures. After reading this book, you may want to find out more about the history of your own first and last names.

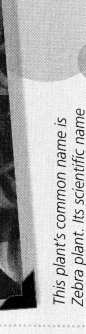

This plant's common name is Zebra plant. Its scientific name is Calathea zebrina.

Namesakes

Names are chosen carefully and often have special meaning. Many children are named after someone their parents **admire.** Your middle name may be your grandmother's given name. You may be named after a friend or a famous person such as a scientist, author, or president.

Were you named after someone else in your family?

Hispanic Naming Traditions

In Hispanic cultures, people have more than one surname, or last name. Many surnames are combinations of both parents' surnames. A boy named Juan López Estaban has both his father's surname (López) and his mother's surname (Estaban).

When a woman marries, she may keep her own surname or add her husband's surname to the end of her own. If she adds his surname, she may link it with a *y*, a hyphen, or *de*, *del*, or *de la* (María Estaban y López).

What would your surname be in the Hispanic tradition?

Surnames and given names have exact meanings in many different cultures.

Given Names for Girls
Deborah (Hebrew) – bee
Afina (Rumanian) – blueberry
Margaret (Latin) – pearl
Bethany (Hebrew) – house

Given Names for Boys
Aran (Thai) – the forest
Oliver (French) – olive tree
Clifford (English) – from a steep cliff
Anwar (African) – the brightest

Surnames
Baker – job
Woods – nature
Fast – quality
Williamson – son of William

Hispanic children have several first names too. José is often one of the given names, or first names, for boys and María is one of the given names for girls.

Many Hispanic families name their children after Catholic saints. Each saint has his or her own feast day. Saint Anthony of Padua's feast day, June 13, is called *El día de San Antonio de Padua*. If a baby boy is born on June 13, the baby's given name may be Antonio.

Many Hispanic children are named after the Catholic saint whose feast day is the same as their birth date.

Exact Meaning

Many people can learn something about their family histories by studying their surnames. Some surnames help identify an ancestor's name. The Swedish name Johnson means "son of John." The prefix, or beginning, of some Irish surnames also gives clues about family relationships. The "O" in O'Callahan means "grandson of." The "Mac" in MacDonald means "son of."

A name can give other information. For example, the surnames Strong and Small give clues to what the people with these names were like. West and Field relate to location and nature. Other surnames, such as Miller, Farmer, and Weaver, describe people's jobs.

Asian Naming Traditions

Traditionally, Chinese, Japanese, Vietnamese, and Korean names begin with the family name, or surname. Have you ever heard of the Chinese basketball player Yao Ming? Yao is his family name. Ming is his given name.

Some Asian given names are based on a theme. For example, in an Indonesian family, three children may be named Intan, which means "diamond," Perak, which means "silver," and Emas, which means "gold."

You might call this basketball player Yao, but that is really his family name. You should call him Ming.

© Pearson Education, Inc.

Nicknames

Nicknames are a popular way to change your name. Many nicknames are short versions of a person's name. Michael may be known as Mike, or Jennifer may like to be called Jenny.

Even pets can have nicknames! Sometimes people show their pets in competitions. The pet may have a long name used just for those events. At home, the pet may be called by a nickname. A pet's name may also be shortened. Pouncer could become Pounce, or Mittens could become Mitt.

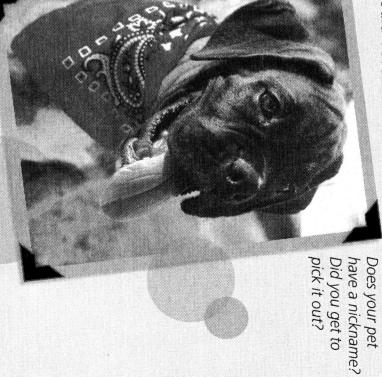

Does your pet have a nickname? Did you get to pick it out?

You may have a middle name that is not used when people speak to you. However, in some Asian countries, more than one word forms a person's given name. For example, Mei Qing Hua means "beautiful blue flower." The entire name must be spoken. To shorten it would change its meaning.

Mei Qing Hua is as pretty as the beautiful blue flower that her mother named her after.

Famous people do not become famous **overnight.** It can take years to become well-known to the **public,** so some entertainers change their names to one that people can remember easily.

Some **popular** musicians change their names to just one word. We know Paul David Hewson as Bono. Madonna Louise Veronica Ciccone put a simple **twist** on her long name by shortening it to Madonna.

Some famous people change or shorten their real names, including Bono and Madonna.

Middle Eastern Naming Traditions

In Jewish families, children may be given both an English name and a Hebrew name. The English name is used every day, while the Hebrew name is used on special occasions.

Another Jewish **custom** is to name children to honor a relative. Boys are usually given their names on the eighth day after their birth. Many parents now hold similar naming ceremonies for their daughters.

In Jewish families, a child's name is very important to his or her future. A baby's name is given eight days after he or she is born.

Changing Names

People change their names for many reasons. When they marry, many American women drop their family names and take their husbands' family names. Other times, the couple may create a last name that combines both of their names. John Stephens and Mary Abbot become John and Mary Stephens Abbot. Sometimes a hyphen is added between the two last names.

When Americans marry, they can choose to keep their own surnames or make up a new one.

12

African Naming Traditions

The Yoruba people of Africa, who live in southwestern Nigeria, also name a child on the eighth day after he or she is born. A Yoruba naming ceremony uses many symbols. The symbols shown on this page are used in the naming ceremony for a baby. The ceremony ends with a feast and party.

money—*The baby is shown money. If he or she reaches for it, he or she will have wealth.*

meat—*The baby is given a small bite of food to remind him or her of all that nature provides.*

water—*Water patted on the baby's face reminds him or her of nature's cleansing qualities.*

oil—*Oil dabbed on the baby's face is to give him or her peace and calm during hard times.*

salt and sugar—*A taste of each is given to improve the baby's sense of taste and bring happiness.*

cola nut—*A taste of cola nut represents a long life.*

ginger—*A taste of ginger symbolizes good health.*

Maori Naming Traditions

Long ago, New Zealand's Maori people performed an ancient ceremony to name a child. People gathered to greet the child and welcome him or her into the world. They brought food as gifts, and there was singing and feasting.

The ceremony took place in a river or stream. People faced east. A priest stood in the water and held the child up to the sky as he said the child's name. Another priest would release a bird and allow it to fly away.

The Maori culture and language is passed on from parents to children.

Haida Naming Traditions

The Queen Charlotte Islands are off the west coast of Canada. The northernmost island, Graham, is home to the Haida people.

Haida objects, including totem poles and button blankets, are decorated with crests. To the Haida people, a crest is like a name. Wherever you go, your crest tells people where you are from and who your relatives are.

A potlatch is a formal ceremony that includes feasting, speeches, singing, dancing, and gif-giving. A special naming potlatch honors the one who is named, and they are given a unique button blanket decorated with the family crest.

The Haida people decorate their totem poles and button blankets with crests that represent a family's history.

The buttons on button blankets were once made from abalone shells. Now mother-of-pearl is used. The Haida believe that the more buttons there are on a blanket, the more power the person who owns the blanket has. One button blanket had more than 1,700 buttons!

Joanie's House Becomes a Home

by Donna Latham
illustrated by Catherine Blake

Suggested levels for Guided Reading, DRA,™
Lexile,® and Reading Recovery™ are provided
in the Pearson Scott Foresman Leveling Guide.

Genre	Comprehension Skills and Strategy	
Realistic fiction	• Sequence • Draw Conclusions • Monitor and Fix Up	

Scott Foresman Reading 3.5.3

ISBN 0-328-13389-2

9 780328 133895

90000

PEARSON

Scott
Foresman

Vocabulary

airport

curious

delicious

described

farewell

homesick

memories

raindrops

Word count: 860

Note: The total word count includes words in the running text and headings only. Numerals and words in chapter titles, captions, labels, diagrams, charts, graphs, sidebars, and extra features are not included.

Reader Response

1. When the Chen family was getting ready to move, what did they do first? Look at page 10, then use a graphic organizer like the one below to record the first three parts of the big move.

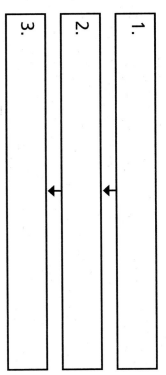

1.

2.

3.

2. As they read, good readers often stop and check to make sure that a text makes sense. Reread page 9. How does Joanie feel about moving?

3. Before the Chens moved, Joanie was not very curious about what her new home and life would be like. Write a list of three antonyms for the word *curious*.

4. A floor plan is a quick and clear way to show the parts of a house. Look at the floor plan on pages 14–15. Name some of the rooms in the Chen's house.

Joanie's House Becomes a Home

by Donna Latham

illustrated by Catherine Blake

Editorial Offices: Glenview, Illinois • Parsippany, New Jersey • New York, New York
Sales Offices: Needham, Massachusetts • Duluth, Georgia • Glenview, Illinois
Coppell, Texas • Ontario, California • Mesa, Arizona

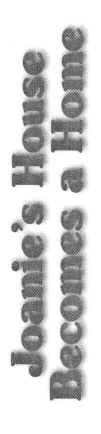

Coast to Coast

The Chens moved from one coast of the United States to another. A coast is a strip of land bordering an ocean. The Pacific Coast, where San Francisco is, runs along the Pacific Ocean. The Atlantic Coast, where Boston is, borders the Atlantic Ocean.

The Chens flew from coast to coast. But what if they had traveled by boat? They would have sailed south along the Pacific Coast to the Panama Canal, in Central America. The canal is about fifty miles long. After sailing through it, they would have continued north along the Atlantic Coast to Boston. How would you rather make the coast-to-coast trip, by plane or by boat?

Every effort has been made to secure permission and provide appropriate credit for photographic material. The publisher deeply regrets any omission and pledges to correct errors called to its attention in subsequent editions.

Unless otherwise acknowledged, all photographs are the property of Scott Foresman, a division of Pearson Education.

ISBN: 0-328-13389-2

"Your room is really comfortable," says Kelly, Joanie's new friend.

"Thanks!" Joanie says. "Now it feels like home. My parents promised we would make this into a real home. But I was too mad about moving to believe them."

"We moved here too—from Texas," Kelly says.

"Don't you get homesick?" asks Joanie.

"Well, it's like what you say. The new house can be homey too. And the ice cream in Boston? Delicious!"

What is a home? It's more than an apartment or a house. A home includes the special things in it. You might have books, toys, and games in your room. You might have a favorite chair in the kitchen. Those things help you feel good.

Sometimes, people need to move to a new home. Moving can be exciting. But it can make you homesick, too.

Let's meet Joanie Chen. She is eight years old. She is packing. Her family is moving to a new city in two days.

Joanie's New Room

Let's see how Joanie's doing. She finished her room. She and her Dad painted the walls yellow and hung up her soccer poster. Her friends from soccer practice in San Francisco sent her a team picture. They signed their names on it. Joanie and her old friends stay in touch with e-mails. She doesn't feel as far away from them as she thought she would.

What else is different about Joanie's room? She's got a new friend visiting.

Packing Up

Joanie and her Mom are packing. But Joanie doesn't want to move. So are my "All my things are here. So are my school and my friends," Joanie says.

"You'll make new friends," Joanie says.

"You'll make new friends," Mrs. Chen says. "And you'll like the new school. We are taking *all* your things. That way, you'll feel right at home."

How are the Chens doing? They've filled their home with their things. Do you think Joanie feels better about her new home now?

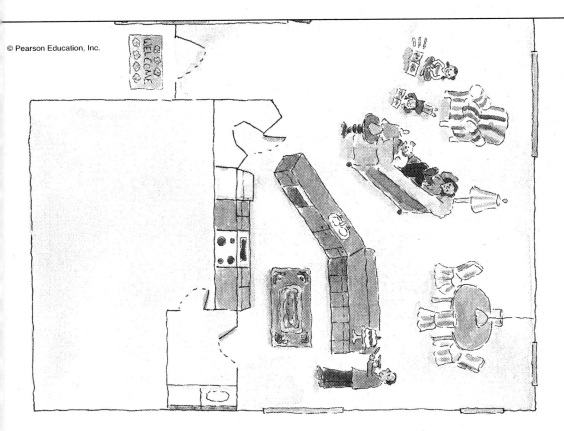

17

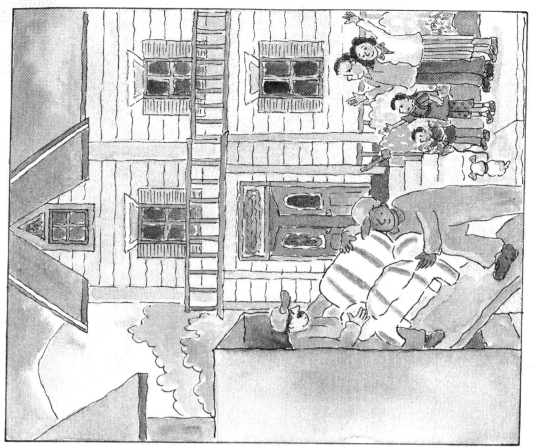

The Chens are saying farewell to their old house in San Francisco, California. They are ready to go. First, they packed all their things into boxes. Now, moving men load the boxes and the furniture into the truck. They empty the entire house.

A New House Becomes a Home

Moving is a big change. You leave your home and you have to start all over again, from scratch. But the moment you bring something of yours into a new place, you're making yourself a home.

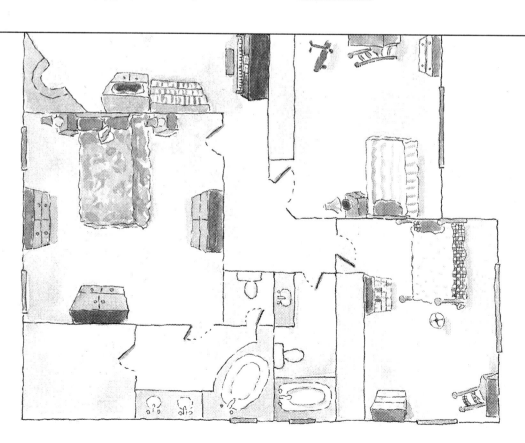

Sometimes people move very far. The Chens are moving all the way from San Francisco, California, to Boston, Massachusetts. That's a move from one side of the United States to the other!

Moving men will drive the truck from California to Massachusetts, right up to the driveway of the Chen's new home. But the Chens are at the airport. They're taking a plane.

The couch, easy chair, piano, bookcase, lamps, and TV go in the living room.

The table, chairs, and ceiling lamp go in the dining room.

The moving men have one day to empty the truck and fill the Chen's whole house. It's a long day!

"I can't wait to see our new home!" says Jimmy.

"I can," says Joanie.

"Aren't you curious what your new home will be like?" her Mom asks.

"Will my bed be there?" Joanie asks.

"It's still in the moving truck," Joanie's Mom says. "The movers will take three days to drive it."

San Francisco to Boston: 3,179 miles

Atlantic Ocean

Boston

Massachusetts

United States

California

San Francisco

Pacific Ocean

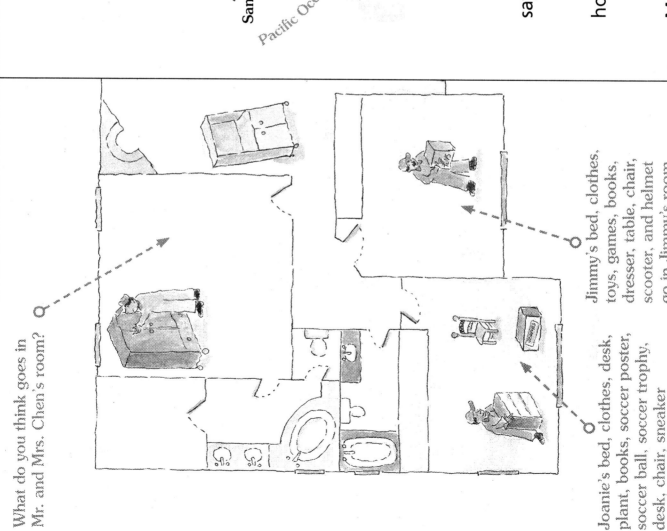

What do you think goes in Mr. and Mrs. Chen's room?

Joanie's bed, clothes, desk, plant, books, soccer poster, soccer ball, soccer trophy, desk, chair, sneaker collection, and photos go in Joanie's room.

Jimmy's bed, clothes, toys, games, books, dresser, table, chair, scooter, and helmet go in Jimmy's room.

Joanie watches raindrops spill down the plane window. She feels sad inside. It started when she was packing. It got stronger at the airport.

She is filled with memories of her San Francisco life. She already misses her school and playing soccer with her friends. She misses the big hills of the city. Most of all, she misses her room, with all her things. She wonders if she'll ever feel at home again.

"Hello Mr. Chen," the moving man says.

"Where do you want your piano?"

"I didn't know we even had a piano!" says Mr. Chen.

"Bring it in the living room please," says Mrs. Chen. "And thanks!"

Where Does This Go?

Did you ever think about where you live? Each room is used in a different way. Every corner of your home plays a part.

We can use a floor plan to see how the Chen's new house is set up. A floor plan is a map of the house, its rooms, walls, and windows. Why is a floor plan important? So you know where to put everything! Mrs. Chen used a floor plan when she described the new house to Joanie.

"This is not a good way to move to a new home," Joanie says to her Mom after some thinking.

"Why?" asks her Mom.

"We don't even have our beds," Joanie says. "What will we sleep on?"

"Don't worry," her Mom says. "We'll pretend we're camping. It'll be fun."

"Right," Joanie says.

CHEN'S BATHROOM

PARENT'S BEDROOM

DINING ROOM

LIVING ROOM

KITCHEN

GARAGE

JIMMY'S BEDROOM

JOANIE'S BEDROOM

CHILDREN'S BATHROOM

First, the Chens packed up their things. Then, moving men packed the boxes and furniture into a truck. The truck is still on the way to Boston. None of the Chen's things will be here for another two days.

"I can't believe this plain empty house is our new home!" says Joanie.

"Don't worry," says Mom. "We will fill it soon enough."

"You bought me a plant!" Joanie says. It makes her happy to see it.

"And when all of our things come we will make this new house into a real home," Mom says.

11

KAPUAPUA'S MAGIC SHELL

by Joe Adair

illustrated by Paula Zinngrabe Wendland

Genre	Comprehension Skills and Strategy
Folktale	• Draw Conclusions • Theme • Summarize

Scott Foresman Reading Street 3.5.4

PEARSON

Scott Foresman

ISBN 0-328-13392-2

9 780328 133925

90000

Vocabulary

bakery

batch

boils

braided

dough

ingredients

knead

mixture

Word count: 1,374

Note: The total word count includes words in the running text and headings only. Numerals and words in chapter titles, captions, labels, diagrams, charts, graphs, sidebars, and extra features are not included.

Reader Response

1. What conclusion can you draw about the villagers at the beginning of the story? Why did they behave the way they did?

2. Summarize the folktale. What lesson does this story teach?

3. Describe the feast. Use as many lesson vocabulary words as you can.

4. How did the villagers change over the course of the story? Use a chart like the one below to record your answers.

Villagers	
Beginning	
Middle	
End	

KAPUAPUA'S MAGIC SHELL

by Joe Adair

illustrated by Paula Zinngrabe Wendland

Editorial Offices: Glenview, Illinois • Parsippany, New Jersey • New York, New York
Sales Offices: Needham, Massachusetts • Duluth, Georgia • Glenview, Illinois
Coppell, Texas • Ontario, California • Mesa, Arizona

A Hawaiian Luau

Kapuapua was a very kind and loving Hawaiian man. He loved to laugh and share his stories with other people. He also loved to eat other people's food!

The feast that we read about in this story is a **luau**. A luau is a Hawaiian term that describes a party with a lot of good food. The roasted pig is cooked underground in a special oven called an *imu*.

Because Hawaii is made up of many islands, there are many kinds of seafood at a luau. Most luaus also have delicious Hawaiian sweet bread. Kapuapua showed the villagers how to make such a dessert.

Luaus also have Hawaiian music and dancing. The story you read gives you a good idea of how much fun a real luau can be!

Kapuapua rested under a palm tree. The wise and loving smile on his face made him look like a benevolent king. The villagers treated him like one, too. They brought him more food and asked him to tell more stories. Kapuapua told them about his exciting adventures on other islands. This gentle and kindly old man with long white hair and a big belly laughed with great joy because he felt just like a king.

Far out in the Pacific Ocean a man sailed his small canoe. The sail caught the wind, and the waves pushed it towards a small island. The island looked tiny because it was so far away.

The man in the canoe was Kapuapua. Kapuapua was an old Hawaiian man who had spent many years sailing from island to island in the Pacific Ocean. He was looking for food and good drinking water. He was hungry and thirsty. The wind hit his sail, and the waves carried him closer to shore.

Everyone was having a wonderful time. They ate the whole roasted pig, all the delicious vegetables, and fresh fruit. The children were playing games as their parents watched and smiled. The young men and women danced all night long to the wonderful music. After the food was eaten, Kapuapua called for the sweet bread to be brought out for dessert. The children were first in line because they loved sweet treats like this.

Kapuapua was a kind and gentle old man. He had long white hair, thick bushy eyebrows, and a big belly. Kapuapua knew many stories. Children loved to sit around him and listen to his stories.

Kapuapua's canoe was getting very close to the shore. He smelled the wonderful aroma coming from the beautiful flowers on the island. He decided that this was an island he wanted to visit.

There was so much food, laughter, dancing, and music. It was wonderful to be at the village for this feast. The weather was just right and everyone sat outside. They ate and talked. Some of the villagers got up and danced. And others gathered around Kapuapua asking him to tell more stories about the places he had visited.

Kapuapua's canoe slid onto the sandy beach. He laughed to himself. He loved being on land again.

Some of the children from the island saw him. They ran to tell their parents about the strange old man. Many of the parents were upset because someone had landed on their island. They believed that this stranger would ask them for food and water. Because he was not one of them, they did not want to share their food or water with him.

The villagers put a table near the soup pot. Next to it they placed the breads, fruit, and the roasted pig. Kapuapua walked over to the huge black pot and tasted some of the soup. He smiled and told everyone that the soup was ready. Then he went and sat back down. But Iz and Howina asked him to be the first to have some of the soup, roasted pig, and fresh fruit. Their feelings for Kapuapua had completely changed. They happily pulled him forward and handed him food. He laughed and filled his big jiggling belly!

Kapuapua smelled cooking food. He followed his nose and ended up at the edge of the village. People saw him and they hid their food.

Kapuapua walked to the first house. A woman named Howina asked him what he wanted. Kapuapua very politely asked for some food and water.

Howina pointed to the stream and said, "You can find water over there, but there is no food in this village." Kapuapua walked over to the stream and drank a lot of water. Now he really needed food.

After the dough was kneaded and braided, the villagers put it in the village oven to bake. Kapuapua told them to take it out when the bread was golden brown. And he told them to sprinkle sugar on top. It was going to be a very delicious dessert.

15

After drinking water, Kapuapua went to the next house. There, he asked for some food. A man named Iz told him to go away. The same thing happened at every house in the village. The people did not want to share food with a stranger.

Soon it became dark and started to rain. No one let this poor old man stay in their home. So Kapuapua fell asleep under a coconut tree.

Kapuapua asked some young men to take over stirring the batch of soup. The pot was getting so full that it was difficult to stir. Other young people of the village began to play wonderful music and dance. Kapuapua could smell the seashell soup and roasting pig in the air. He smiled and watched as other villagers cut up pineapples and other fruit. Then he walked over to the men and women making the dough for the sweet bread. He showed them how to knead it. Then he told them to make it into long logs and braid it together.

The next morning Kapuapua felt something hit his head. It was a coconut that fell from the tree. It hurt a little, but it gave him a wonderful idea!

Kapuapua had a plan to get food from the villagers. He needed his magic seashell though. So he walked back to the beach and took the seashell out of his canoe.

Kapuapua walked to the center of the village and began to make a fire under a large black cooking pot.

Some young people asked Kapuapua if they could taste his soup if they danced and played music. Again, his big, round stomach jiggled as he laughed loudly and said yes!

Kapuapua then asked the villagers if they had a bakery. They didn't know what he meant. So he told the villagers about a good sweet bread they should make for dessert. Some of the villagers asked how to make it. Kapuapua told them how to make the dough for the bread.

13

Kapuapua lit a fire and poured water from the stream into the big pot. Howina asked him what he was doing. He told her he was making his magic seashell soup.

"Magic seashell soup. Whatever in the world is that?" Howina asked.

He laughed. Soon the children joined her. Kapuapua explained that many years ago he met a famous king and went to a great feast with him. Kapuapua cooked his magic seashell soup for the king. The king loved it!

Soon the whole village was lined up with all sorts of delicious seafoods, green vegetables, and sweet fruits. Kapuapua added them to the pot.

He told them about the man at the king's party who roasted a whole pig for the party. Just then a man from the village said, "I have a pig. If I roast it for the villagers, will you let me taste the magic seashell soup?" Kapuapua said yes and continued with his story. He told them about men and women who sang beautiful songs and played lovely music.

Kapuapua picked up the seashell. He was the only one who knew it was just a regular shell that he found a long time ago. He dropped it into the water. A little splash jumped from the pot and landed on the back of his hand. The people watched as he licked his hand. Then he said, "Mmm, this soup is going to be great!"

Soon the villagers begged for a taste. Kapuapua told them they could have a taste if they added other ingredients to the pot. They asked what they could add to the mixture. Kapuapua asked Iz to bring some fish and Howina to get some nice green vegetables for the soup.

Kapuapua continued with the story. He told the villagers, "As soon as the water boils, I will make a pot of magic soup." But, he told them, they could not have any of his soup. There was only enough for one person.

Soon the villagers asked if they could add some food of their own. Then there would be enough for them to taste. Kapuapua just smiled and kept on stirring.

Bobby's New Apartment

by Jason Lublinski

illustrated by Alexandra Leff

Genre	Comprehension Skills and Strategy
Realistic fiction	• Author's Purpose • Realism and Fantasy • Prior Knowledge

Scott Foresman Reading Street 3.5.5

ISBN 0-328-13395-7

90000

9 780328 133956

PEARSON

Scott Foresman

Vocabulary

cardboard

feast

fierce

flights

pitcher

ruined

stoops

treasure

Word count: 1,350

Note: The total word count includes words in the running text and headings only. Numerals and words in chapter titles, captions, labels, diagrams, charts, graphs, sidebars, and extra features are not included.

Reader Response

1. What purpose do you think the author had for telling this story?

2. What do you know about living in an apartment building? How is it different from living in a house? Make a diagram like the one below to show how the two are alike and different.

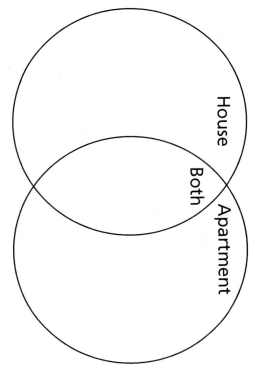

House   Both   Apartment

3. On page 13, a new meaning of the word "super" is introduced. How else can you use the word super?

4. How does Jose help make moving into the apartment easier for Bobby?

Bobby's New Apartment

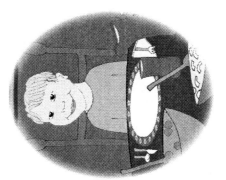

by Jason Lublinski
illustrated by Alexandra Leff

Editorial Offices: Glenview, Illinois • Parsippany, New Jersey • New York, New York
Sales Offices: Needham, Massachusetts • Duluth, Georgia • Glenview, Illinois
Carroll, Texas • Ontario, California • Mesa, Arizona

Apartment Life

It takes a lot of work to take care of a building. It also takes a lot of people.

The super makes sure everything is fixed. He or she is also in charge of trash pickup. Sometimes there is also a maintenance person to help the super.

If there is a problem with the elevator, the super can call an elevator repair person. If there is a problem with the plumbing, the super can call a plumber.

Some apartment buildings also have people working at the door. They announce visitors and take packages. They may also help the older people who live in the building. They may carry their grocery bags when they come in.

3

Copyright © Pearson Education, Inc.

ISBN: 0-328-13395-7

Bobby Waters and his parents stood in front of their new home. They had just moved from their house in a small town to the big city. Their new home was an apartment building. It rose into the sky. All Bobby could see was row after row of windows.

"What a big building," Bobby's father said. "Must be 50 flights of stairs. Maybe a hundred apartments."

That made Bobby scared. "How many people live here?" he asked. "I guess we won't have a front stoop like we had before."

That night, Bobby sat down to dinner with his parents. Outside the big picture window, he could see the lights from all the apartments across the street. So many people lived all around! It was so different from living in a house. In some ways, Bobby thought he liked it. He thought he would never feel alone.

Inside, the apartment was beginning to feel like home. His parents had stayed up late unpacking boxes. They set up furniture and put out plants. His father had even cooked macaroni and cheese, his next-favorite food, for dinner. But they did not have to drive to the store for groceries. They just went down the elevator and walked down the block.

His mother poured him some milk from a pitcher and smiled. "Know what?" he said to her. "I think I'm going to like living in an apartment after all."

A tall man in a fancy uniform came out of the building. "Hello, Waters family!" he said. He stood in a way that looked like he was leaning over. He looked a little fierce to Bobby.

"Say hello to Ron, our doorman," Bobby's mother said. "He watches this building. He lets us know if we have visitors or packages.

"Visitors?" Bobby said. "We don't even know anyone." Bobby missed his house and his friends already.

"In this building, we need to help each other out," Jose said to Bobby as they headed downstairs. "It's like a small town." Bobby liked that idea.

They got into the elevator. It looked like there were a hundred buttons. Each one was a different floor. "We live on the 21st floor," Bobby's mother said. "Isn't that exciting?"

"I don't think so," Bobby said. The elevator began to rise. It made his stomach feel funny. It felt like they were rising very, very high.

"Look! I found a key to a treasure box on the ground," Jose said. He held it up. It was the smallest key Bobby had ever seen.

"That's a mailbox key," Jose's father said. "Someone must have lost it. We should give it to Ron so he can get it back to its owner."

The elevator stopped. Bobby started to get out. "Not yet," his mother said. "This isn't our floor." A little girl and her mother got in. The girl looked at Bobby.

This place is so strange, Bobby thought. *I wonder if people ever talk to each other around here.* "Mom," Bobby said, "do people talk in the elevators here?"

The little girl's mother burst out laughing. "You must be new to the building," the woman said. "I'm Mrs. Low, and this is Hazel. She loves to talk."

"There's a big fence," Jose said, laughing.

They went up to the roof. It was as big as a whole block! Bobby could not believe his eyes. Children played on swings and in the sandbox. They climbed on a jungle gym. Parents were sitting around on benches. There were trees and grass! It was like a park up in the sky. Around the whole playground was a high fence. It looked very strong.

Bobby's mother smiled and said, "I'm Jean Waters, and this is Bobby. He likes to talk, too."

"We used to live in a big house with lots of rooms," Bobby said sadly.

"I bet you miss your house," Mrs. Low said to Bobby. "Soon you might like living in a very big building with many, many rooms," Mrs. Low said.

"We live in 33D," said Hazel. "Where do you live?"

"I don't know yet. We just moved in," Bobby said. "You could come with us and see our new apartment," Bobby said with a smile.

"Maybe sometime soon, Bobby," Mrs. Low said. "Hazel and I need to have lunch now. Maybe you and your mom could come and have cookies with us later?"

In the laundry room, Bobby saw more washing machines and dryers than he'd ever seen in one place. A man folded clothes at a big table. A little boy was riding his bike around the room. "Hey!" the boy said to Bobby. "Who are you?" "Who are you?" Bobby said.

"I'm Jose," the boy said. "We live in 22D."

"Bobby. 21B," Bobby said. "How old are you? I'm eight."

"Me too!" said Jose. "Got a bike?" he said. "Want to race?"

"Sure!" said Bobby. His father helped him get his bike from the bike room. Then Jose and Bobby raced up and down the long basement hall. "I could never do this in my old place," Bobby said as he whizzed past Jose. "I always had to watch out for cars. This is so much better!"

When they were done riding bikes, Jose and his father joined the tour of the building. "Let's go to the roof," Jose said. "There's a playground up there."

"A playground on the roof?" Bobby said. "I never heard of such a thing. What if you fall off the edge?"

The elevator bumped to a stop. "Here we are," said Bobby's mother. They walked down a long hallway. It smelled like chicken soup. All the doors were the same color—brown.

The Waters' apartment was 21B. It was empty except for boxes and suitcases. Sunlight poured in the windows. The walls were just painted. The floors were covered with cardboard.

"The blue bins are for glass. The green bins are for newspapers. The white bins are for trash. Then the super brings it out for pickup."

"Super?" Bobby said. "Like a super hero?"

Bobby's father laughed. "Kind of," he said. "Super is short for superintendent. He takes care of this whole building. That's his job."

"Like you and Mommy took care of our house?" Bobby said. "But this building is huge! It must have 200 apartments. What a big job!"

"Wow!" Bobby said, sliding across the cardboard. "Why is this on the floors?"

"So they wouldn't be ruined when the painters worked," Bobby's mother said.

Bobby liked the smell of fresh paint. He looked out the window at the street far below. It made him feel dizzy to be so high up.

The next day, Bobby's father took him on a tour of the building. "I want you to know your way around," his father said. "This building is so big it's like a small city."

"Sure is," Bobby said.

First they got in the elevator. "Press B," Bobby's father said. "B is for basement," he explained. "But you are not to come down here by yourself."

"I promise," Bobby said. "It's scary!"

The basement was huge. There were rooms everywhere. One had bicycles in it. Another had mops and buckets. Another had giant trash bins. "That's where we take the garbage," Bobby's father said.

That night, the Waters ordered pizza. Bobby loved pizza. It would be a feast! Soon, a loud buzzer sounded. "What was that?" Bobby said from his room. He was putting his toys and books on the bookcase. His new room was much bigger than his old room.

"The lobby phone," his mother called.

"The what?" Bobby called back.

"The lobby is a name for the first floor," his father said. "Ron called to tell us to go downstairs and pick up the pizza. Want to go?"

"Why can't the pizza man just come upstairs?" Bobby said.

"It makes it safer this way," Bobby's mother said.

On the way downstairs, Bobby got to press the buttons himself. He even got to hold the money. "We just moved in!" he said to anyone he saw. "We got pizza for dinner!" Everyone laughed.

Social Studies

Signs, Songs, and Symbols of America

by Alma Ransford

Genre	Comprehension Skills and Strategy	Text Features
Expository nonfiction	• Main Idea and Details • Fact and Opinion • Text Structure	• Captions • Headings

Scott Foresman Reading Street 3.6.1

PEARSON

Scott Foresman

ISBN 0-328-13398-1

9 780328 133987

90000

Vocabulary

crown

liberty

models

symbol

tablet

torch

unforgettable

unveiled

Word count: 1,278

Reader Response

1. What is the main idea of the section called Our Nation's Songs? Tell two details that support the main idea. Use a graphic organizer like this one.

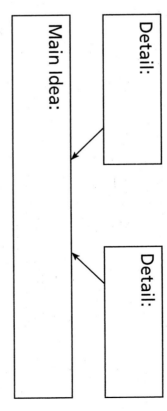

Main Idea:

Detail:

Detail:

2. How do the headings prepare you for what is coming next in the selection? Give an example.

3. Two of the glossary words begin with the same prefix. Name the words and identify the prefix. What other words do you know that begin with that prefix? Name two and use each in a sentence.

4. Why do you think the scene described on page 6 inspired Francis Scott Key? Would it have inspired you? Why or why not?

Signs, Songs, and Symbols of America

by Alma Ransford

PEARSON

Scott
Foresman

Editorial Offices: Glenview, Illinois • Parsippany, New Jersey • New York, New York
Sales Offices: Needham, Massachusetts • Duluth, Georgia • Glenview, Illinois
Carroll, Texas • Ontario, California • New Jersey

Glossary

crown *n.* head covering of precious metals worn by a king or queen.

liberty *n.* freedom.

models *n.* small scale copies of objects.

symbol *n.* something that stands for something else.

tablet *n.* a flat surface with an inscription, or message, carved into it or placed upon it.

torch *n.* portable light produced by lighting material fastened to the end of a stick.

unforgettable *adj.* not able to be forgotten.

unveiled *v.* removed a covering from.

Photo locators denoted as follows: Top (T), Center (C), Bottom (B), Left (L), Right (R), Background (Bkgd)

Opener (TL) © Leif Skoogfors/Corbis, Opener (BR) ©Bill Ross/Corbis, Opener (CL) ©Francis G. Mayer/Corbis; 1 (R) ©Jeff Vanuga/Corbis, 1 (L) © Leif Skoogfors/Corbis; 3 ©Patrick Roncen/Corbis; 4 ©Bruce Burkhardt/Corbis; 5 (TR) ©Royalty-Free/Corbis, 5 (B) ©Francis G. Mayer/Corbis; 6 ©Corbis; 7 ©Bettmann/Corbis; 8 ©Dean Conger/Corbis; 9 ©Bettmann/Corbis; 10 (L) ©Jeff Vanuga/Corbis, 10 (R) ©Ralph A. Clevenger/Corbis; 11 © Swim Ink 2, LLC/Corbis; 12 ©Free Agents Limited/Dallas and John Heaton /Corbis; 13 ©Bill Ross/Corbis; 14 © John & Dallas Heaton/Corbis; 15 ©Adam Woolfitt/Corbis; 16 ©Galen Rowell/Corbis; 17 (TL) ©Peter Finger/Corbis, 17 (TR) © James P. Blair/Corbis; 18 © Leif Skoogfors/Corbis

ISBN: 0-328-13398-1

Copyright © Pearson Education, Inc.

2 3 4 5 6 7 8 9 10 V0G1 14 13 12 11 10 09 08 07 06 05

Our Nation's Creed and Mottos

Our nation has an official creed and motto. The Creed reads in part, "I believe in the United States of America as a

government of the people, by the people, for the people...."

Since 1956, the motto of the United States has been "In God We Trust." The government also recognized the phrase *E Pluribus Unum*, which appears on the Great Seal. Since 1963, Congress has used both as our national mottos.

The Liberty Bell first rang out in 1776 to announce the Declaration of Independence.

© Pearson E

A **symbol** is something that stands for something else. For example, if you see a sign with an "H" on it, you know a hospital is nearby. Symbols are all around us. There are many different types of symbols. Your school may have a mascot or special school colors. Symbols give us information, but they can also stand for ideas and ideals.

Symbols can be signs, flags and pennants, animals, or just colors.

Our Nation's Liberty Bell

Philadelphia, Pennsylvania, is home to the Liberty Bell. It was hung in the state house in Philadelphia in 1753. The bell was rung on July 8, 1776, to celebrate the first public reading of the Declaration of Independence. It was rung for the last time on George Washington's birthday in 1846, when its famous crack became so large that it could not be fixed.

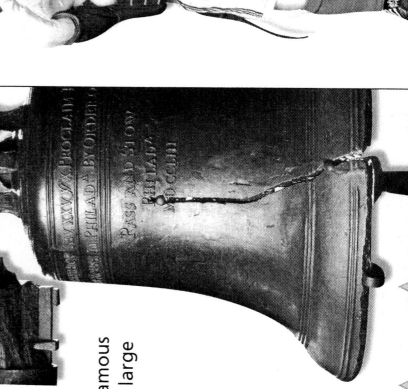

Symbols of America

In the United States, we have many symbols that stand for things our nation holds dear. Some of them are official symbols of our country. The flag and the bald eagle are two examples. Others are popular symbols that we use, see, or sing all the time. Some of these popular symbols are the Statue of **Liberty,** our national anthem, and the White House.

What symbols of the United States can you think of?

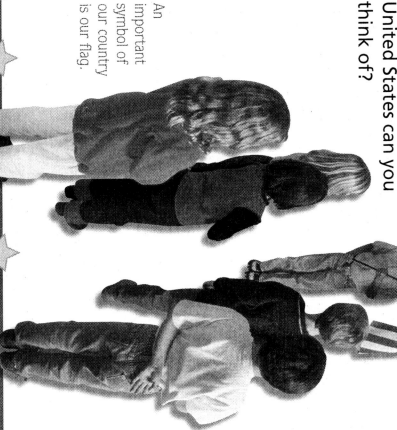

An important symbol of our country is our flag.

The Vietnam Veterans Memorial

The Korean War Memorial

Many monuments throughout the country symbolize accomplishments of past leaders. The Jefferson Memorial, the Washington Memorial, and the Lincoln Memorial are all located in Washington, D.C. Each of them honors the President for whom it's named.

We also recognize the brave sacrifices our soldiers have made during times of war. We have memorials to those who fought in World War II, the Korean War, and the Vietnam War. These memorials are also in Washington, D.C.

The White House is the official home of the President. Although much about it has changed, it actually looks much as it did when it was first built in 1800.

James Hoban won the competition for the building's design in 1792. He envisioned a first or "state" floor where public business would take place. The President's family would live on the second floor. Over time, the White House has had several additions.

The White House

Our Nation's Flag

One of our country's official symbols is the American flag. Legend says that Betsy Ross of Pennsylvania sewed the first flag for our new nation. The Continental Congress adopted the national flag on June 14, 1777.

Charles Thomson, secretary of the Continental Congress, said the flag was to be red (for hardiness and valor), white (for innocence), and blue (for vigilance, perseverance, and justice).

As new states enter the Union, stars are added. The thirteen stripes remain to remind us of the original thirteen colonies.

Betsy Ross shows the first American flag to General Washington.

Our Nation's Songs

The American flag inspired Francis Scott Key to write the song that became our national anthem. Key watched the British attack Fort McHenry during the War of 1812. The attack went on all night. It seemed impossible that the fort could survive the bombardment by the British army and navy.

Yet early the next morning, Key looked at the fort through the dim light of dawn. The American flag was still waving over the fort. Thrilled by the sight, Key wrote a poem about it.

Francis Scott Key

The United States Supreme Court Building

Thomas Jefferson was the first President to be inaugurated, or sworn into office, at the Capitol. This is a tradition that continues to this day. The original Capitol building burned during the War of 1812, but later it was rebuilt.

The poem began:

Oh, say can you see, by the
dawn's early light
What so proudly we hailed at
the twilight's last gleaming?

The poem was set to music. "The Star-Spangled Banner" became our official national anthem in 1931.

Over the years, other songs have come to symbolize the United States. "America the Beautiful" by Katharine Lee Bates is nearly as popular as the national anthem.

Battle at Fort McHenry

Our Nation's Government Buildings

Three important symbols of our national government are the White House, the U.S. Supreme Court building, and the U.S. Capitol building. The U.S. Supreme Court hears the most important cases in the nation in the Supreme Court building. The White House is home to the President of the United States. The Capitol building is the meeting place of the U.S. Congress.

Senators and members of the House of Representatives make our laws in the U.S. Capitol.

Composer George M. Cohan met a Civil War veteran who inspired him to write one of his most popular songs. The man was carrying a very carefully folded flag. Cohan wrote "You're a Grand Old Flag" as a tribute to the flag and to the man who so proudly carried it.

Another important song that symbolizes our country is "Hail to the Chief." It is the official anthem of the President and has been since 1954. It accompanies the President at most every public event.

Patriotic songs and music symbolize pride in our country.

Poet Emma Lazarus wrote a poem, "The New Colossus," in 1883, before the statue was **unveiled**. The poem was placed on a bronze plaque at the base of the statue. The statue symbolizes the poem's message of hope, freedom, and democracy.

Our Nation's Statue of Freedom

The Statue of Liberty is one of the United States' most famous symbols. The people of France gave the statue to the people of the United States in 1886 to celebrate the friendship between the two nations.

The statue was designed by Frederic Bartholdi. He made several **models** for each of its major parts. In Lady Liberty's **crown** are seven rays representing the seven seas and continents of the world. In her right hand is a **torch** lighting the way to America. The **tablet** in her left hand has the date July 4, 1776, in Roman numerals. That is the date of the Declaration of Independence.

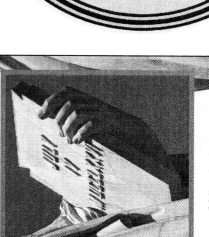

For more than one hundred years, the Statue of Liberty has welcomed immigrants to the United States.

Our Nation's Official Seal

On July 4, 1776, the Continental Congress authorized design of a "device for a seal of the United States of America." William Barton and Charles Thomson created the design.

The design was approved by Congress in 1782. The seal includes the American bald eagle with a ribbon in its mouth. On the ribbon are the Latin words *E Pluribus Unum*, which means "out of many, one." In the eagle's left talon, or claw, are thirteen arrows, representing war. In the right talon is an olive branch, representing peace.

The Great Seal of the United States is used on all official documents.

The bald eagle has been the national bird since 1782. It is a symbol of our nation's freedom. It appears in many places. You'll find it on the President's flag, on the Great Seal, and on the one-dollar bill.

If Benjamin Franklin had had his way, our national bird would be the wild turkey. Franklin argued that the wild turkey was native to America and a very intelligent bird. He lost the argument.

The bald eagle is our national bird. It stands for freedom.

Our Nation's Uncle Sam

Another **unforgettable** symbol that uses the colors red, white, and blue is Uncle Sam. He is usually pictured as a tall man with white hair, a small white beard, and dressed in a star-spangled suit.

Samuel Wilson, a beef supplier in Troy, New York, probably inspired the idea for Uncle Sam. During the War of 1812, he supplied barrels of beef to the U.S. Army. He stamped them "U.S." to show that they were government property. People think this led to the use of the nickname "Uncle Sam" to symbolize the United States.

This cartoon of Uncle Sam was used during World War II to persuade men to join the armed forces.

Life Science

Science

Science

Caring for Your Pet Bird

by Lana Cruce

Genre	Comprehension Skills and Strategy	Text Features
Expository nonfiction	• Cause and Effect • Main Idea • Graphic Organizers	• Captions • Glossary • List • Sidebars

Scott Foresman Reading Street 3.6.2

PEARSON

Scott Foresman

ISBN 0-328-13401-5

9 780328 134014

90000

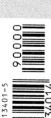

Vocabulary

bows

chilly

foolish

foreign

narrow

perches

recipe

Word count: 1,360

Note: The total word count includes words in the running text and headings only. Numerals and words in chapter titles, captions, labels, diagrams, charts, graphs, sidebars, and extra features are not included.

Reader Response

1. What can happen if you and your family are very busy and your bird lives alone in its cage?

2. On a separate piece of paper, copy the chart below. In the first column, list some things you need to do before you bring your bird home. In the second column, list some things you need to do after you bring your bird home.

Things to Do Before You Bring Your Bird Home	Things to Do After You Bring Your Bird Home

3. What is another word for cold that you learned from this selection? Write it on your paper. Use a dictionary to find a word that means the opposite. Use each in a sentence.

4. Which bird in this selection is small, has orange feet and a red beak, and likes company? Which bird is your favorite? Why?

Caring for Your Pet Bird

by Lana Cruce

PEARSON
Scott
Foresman

Editorial Offices: Glenview, Illinois • Parsippany, New Jersey • New York, New York
Sales Offices: Needham, Massachusetts • Duluth, Georgia • Glenview, Illinois

Glossary

bows *v.* bends the head or body

chilly *adj.* cold

foolish *adj.* ridiculous or silly

foreign *adj.* from a country other than your own

narrow *adj.* not very wide

perches *n.* hanging bars for a bird to sit or rest on

recipe *n.* a set of instructions for making something using certain ingredients

Every effort has been made to secure permission and provide appropriate credit for photographic material. The publisher deeply regrets any omission and pledges to correct errors called to its attention in subsequent editions.

Unless otherwise acknowledged, all photographs are the property of Scott Foresman, a division of Pearson Education.

Photo locators denoted as follows: Top (T), Center (C), Bottom (B), Left (L), Right (R), Background (Bkgd)

Cover ©Catherine Karnow/CORBIS; 1 ©Tom & Dee Ann McCarthy/CORBIS; 3 ©Chris Jones/CORBIS; 4 ©B. Franklin/CORBIS; 5 ©Fine Art Photographic Library/CORBIS; 6(L) ©DK Limited/CORBIS; 6(R) ©DK Limited/CORBIS; 9 ©Steve Gorton/ Dorling Kindersley Media Library; 10 ©Staffan Widstrand/CORBIS; 11 ©ROB ELLIOTT/AFP/Getty Images; 13 ©Ralph A. Clevenger/CORBIS; 14 ©Bob Rowan; Progressive Image/CORBIS; 15 ©Catherine Karnow/CORBIS; 16 ©Ted Horowitz/CORBIS; 17(L) ©Eric and David Hosking/CORBIS; 17(R) ©DK Limited/CORBIS; 18 ©Tom & Dee Ann McCarthy/CORBIS; 19 ©Reuters/CORBIS

ISBN: 0-328-13401-5

2 3 4 5 6 7 8 9 10 V0G1 14 13 12 11 10 09 08 07 06 05

A veterinarian can be your pet's most important friend.

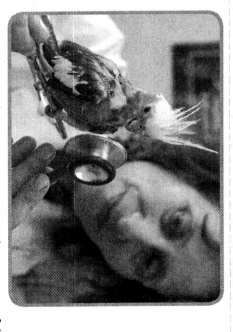

Although birds are usually very healthy, sometimes they can get sick. For example, if a bird is sneezing and keeping its feathers ruffled, it may have a cold. If it is scratching itself, it may have mites. If your bird is acting different from the way it usually acts, talk to a veterinarian.

Every year, usually in the summer, birds molt. This means that they shed their old feathers and grow new ones. If your bird is molting, you do not need to worry or take it to the vet.

If you keep your pet bird clean, warm, and well fed; talk to it and play with it every day; and take it to the vet if it becomes sick, you will have a healthy, happy pet for a very long time!

Birds make wonderful pets. They are beautiful. Some are very smart. Most are very loving. People have been keeping birds as pets for thousands of years. Today, pet birds are still popular pets.

Having a pet bird is a lot of fun, but it is also a big responsibility. It takes work, understanding, patience, and lots of love to have a happy pet bird.

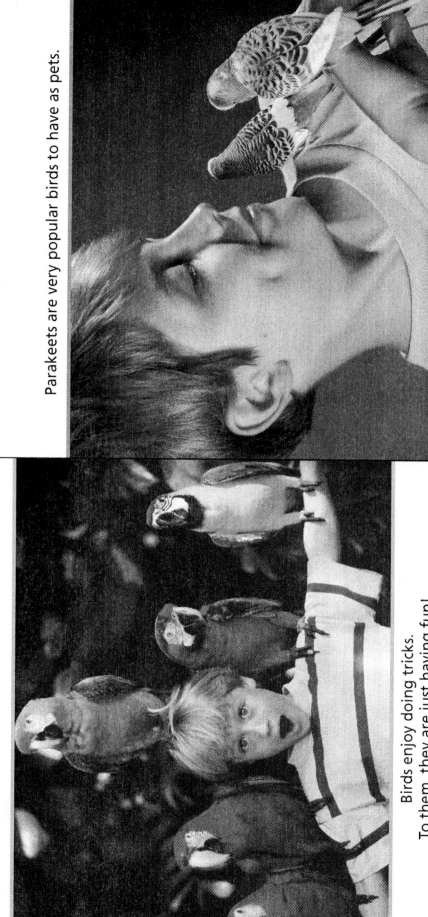

Parakeets are very popular birds to have as pets.

Training Your Pet Bird

Some birds can be trained to do tricks and even to talk. A well-trained bird repeats words, throws a ball into a cup, and **bows** its head when you clap.

You can use books, Web sites, and magazines to find out how to train your bird. Remember, the most important rule is always to be gentle and patient with your bird.

Birds enjoy doing tricks.
To them, they are just having fun!

Choosing a Pet Bird

Many birds were once brought from **foreign** countries. Today, it is illegal to bring birds from many countries. Taking wild birds out of their natural habitat can make them become endangered. You should buy only birds that are bred and raised here in the United States.

All species of parrots come from places with warm climates, such as Mexico, Central America, and South America.

Lovebirds like to live in pairs.

Canaries like to live alone.

Birds can also get lonely. In the wild, most birds live in flocks with many other birds. If you have a lot of time to give to your bird, it will be happy living alone in its cage. If you are gone most of the day, it may be a good idea to get more than one bird. But first make sure that your bird will get along well with another bird. (Ask a vet.)

There are many types of birds that people keep as pets. Some people think that birds in the parrot family make the best pets. These birds include parakeets, cockatiels, lovebirds, conures, and macaws. They are very intelligent, loving, and usually have long lives. You can teach them to do tricks and even to talk.

Like their owners, birds have feelings. Most birds are very smart and have good memories. If they are treated badly, they will remember it and start to behave badly.

Always be gentle and kind to your pet bird. Never hit it or yell at it. Hitting or yelling will scare your bird. It may even try to bite you.

Some people think it's cute to dress their pet birds in doll clothes. This is not a good idea. It will confuse your bird and may make it feel **foolish.**

Treat your bird well, and it will trust you and behave well.

Some types of finches also make good pets. Many people keep chirpy zebra finches as pets. They are very small birds with orange feet and bright red beaks. Zebra finches should be kept in pairs so that they won't get lonely.

Canaries are another popular pet. The male canary has a lovely singing voice. Although canaries come in many colors, the most common canary color is bright yellow. Unlike zebra finches, canaries like to live alone.

A canary

A pair of zebra finches

Your bird needs quiet time when you first bring it home. Do not try to pet or handle your bird right away. Keep your bird in its cage. Don't let it fly around the house for the first few weeks. Your bird needs to relax and get used to its new home.

Speak gently and quietly to your bird. Do not make any loud, sudden noises that will frighten it.

Getting Ready for Your Pet Bird

Before you bring your pet bird home, you need to have a place for it to live. You need to get a cage. The cage should be large enough so that the bird can hold on to the bars and easily flap its wings. Cages with a rectangular shape are best. The bars should be spaced so that the bird can't poke its head between them.

Making a comfortable home for your bird is important to its health and happiness.

Loving Your Pet Bird

It is very important to meet your pet bird's physical needs. It is just as important to let your bird know that you love it and that it can trust you. Birds can become sick from stress. This usually happens when a bird is a new pet. Your bird must adjust to its new surroundings and get to know you.

Bird Care Tips

★ Keep the bird in a warm room.

★ Feed your bird food it is used to eating.

★ Give your bird twelve hours of quiet and darkness each day.

★ Do not handle your bird for the first few weeks.

★ Except during playtime, keep the bird in its cage.

★ Avoid loud noises around your bird.

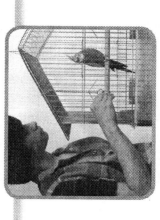

It is very important to give your new pet time to get used to you, your family, and its new home.

Your bird should have several different **perches** in its cage. This will allow the bird to stretch and change positions on perches of different sizes and shapes. Remember, your bird will stand on its perches twenty-four hours a day.

For your bird's comfort, be sure that the perch is neither too **narrow** nor too wide. The perch is the right size if your bird's toes just barely go around it. The perch should be made from edible wood so that your bird can chew on it. Some birds need to chew on things so that the upper parts of their beaks do not grow too long.

Your bird also needs toys. Playing with toys gives birds exercise, as well as something to chew on.

If you cut your own wood to make a perch, bake it in the oven at low heat for 30 to 45 minutes. Then you can put it in the cage. Baking it will kill any insects that may have been inside the wood.

It is also important that your bird gets sunlight. But never put it in hot, direct sunlight for a long time. Birds can become overheated easily. A good solution may be to get a special light, called a full-spectrum bird light. This light is good for your bird, but it is not dangerous.

At night you should cover your bird's cage with a sheet or a towel. Your bird should have ten to twelve hours of total quiet and darkness each day.

A warm bird is a happy bird!

Many birds like bells, mirrors, light balls, rings, and swings. All bird toys should be safe to chew on. Your bird's toys should hang from chains, not from string. String can get tangled around your bird's feet or neck.

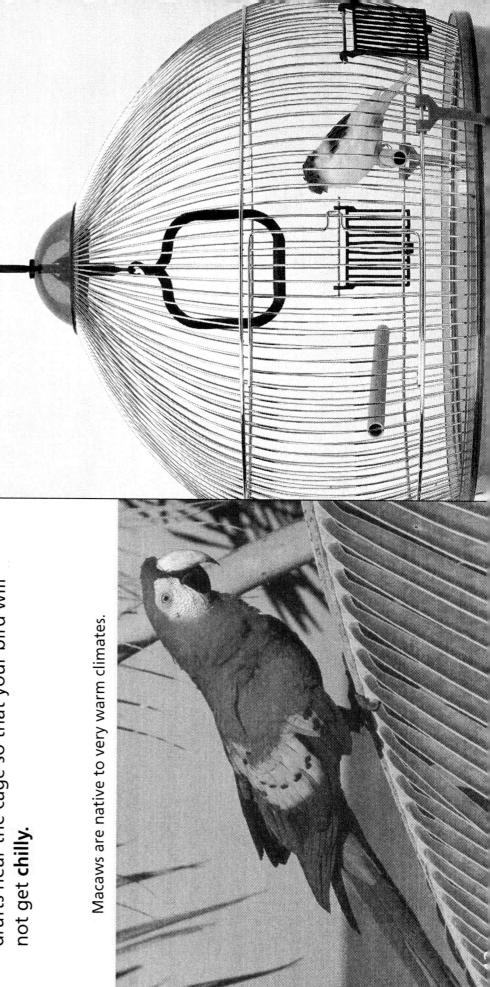

Keeping Your Pet Bird Warm

It is important to keep your bird warm. Most birds are from warm climates and don't like cold. This is especially important when you first bring your bird home. For the first few days, try to keep the room where your bird is kept slightly warmer than usual. Make sure there are no cold drafts near the cage so that your bird will not get **chilly.**

Macaws are native to very warm climates.

Feeding Your Pet Bird

Before you bring home a pet bird, you will need to know the right kind of food to feed it. Your veterinarian or pet store owner can help you find the exact kind of food to feed your particular bird. They can also help you find the right **recipe** to make your own bird food.

Most pet birds like the challenge of finding food. Birds are naturally curious creatures. Give them different treats, such as apples, carrots, and corn. Place the treats in different parts of the cage so your pet can hunt for them.

Feeding your bird is a good way to show you care!

Taking Care of Your Pet Bird

Your bird should have fresh water every day. You should also change the newspaper at the bottom of its cage every day. The cage must be kept clean, so the bird can stay healthy.

Some birds like to take baths. You can put a shallow dish of water in the cage every week. Remove the dish when the bird is finished bathing.

Your bird should also have a dish of grit in its cage. Grit is small stones that a bird uses to grind its food, since it does not have teeth. It is also a good idea to attach a piece of mineral block to the side of the cage. Your bird needs minerals, such as calcium. It can get these from pecking the mineral block.

Never place dishes with food, treats, water, or grit directly under a bird's perch. This will protect them from getting soiled by your bird.

A Whole World in One City

by Juliette Ruiz

Suggested levels for Guided Reading, DRA,™ Lexile,® and Reading Recovery™ are provided in the Pearson Scott Foresman Leveling Guide.

Genre	Comprehension Skills and Strategy
Realistic fiction	• Fact and Opinion • Compare and Contrast • Monitor and Fix Up

Scott Foresman Reading Street 3.6.3

ISBN 0-328-13404-X

9 780328 134045

90000

PEARSON

Scott Foresman

Vocabulary

encourages

expression

local

native

settled

social

support

Word count: 1,185

Reader Response

1. Look back through the story, concentrating on the characters' speeches. Find two statements of fact and two statements of opinion in what they say. Write them in the chart.

Fact	Opinion

2. Did you have questions as you read? How did you answer those questions?

3. Make a list of non-English words you learned from the story. Write the language and what the words mean.

4. Do you think Lily's family is unique in wanting to explore ethnic neighborhoods? Why or why not?

A Whole World in One City

by Juliette Ruiz
illustrated by Bill Peterson

PEARSON
Scott
Foresman

Editorial Offices: Glenview, Illinois • Parsippany, New Jersey • New York, New York
Sales Offices: Needham, Massachusetts • Duluth, Georgia • Glenview, Illinois

Ethnic Neighborhoods

Most cities, and many small towns across the United States are home to "ethnic" communities. These are communities where people from a particular culture have settled. Did you know that Chicago has an old Swedish neighborhood called Andersonville? Chicago's Lincoln Square was home to a large German-American population and still celebrates German heritage days. Chicago also has a Greektown that is home to the world's third largest Greek community.

Some of these communities can change over time. The Mexican community of Pilsen first started out as a community of Czechoslovakian people who came from the Czech city of Pilsen.

See if you can locate some of these nations or regions on a world map.

ISBN: 0-328-13404-X

Copyright © Pearson Education, Inc.

All Rights Reserved. Printed in the United States of America. This publication is protected by Copyright, and permission should be obtained from the publisher prior to any prohibited reproduction, storage in a retrieval system, or transmission in any form by any means, electronic, mechanical, photocopying, recording, or likewise. For information regarding permission(s), write to: Permissions Department, Scott Foresman, 1900 East Lake Avenue, Glenview, Illinois 60025.

1 2 3 4 5 6 7 8 9 10 V0G1 14 13 12 11 10 09 08 07 06 05

Lily Sung stared out the window of her new home in Chicago. "We're so lucky to be here," said Lily's mom. But Lily didn't feel lucky.

She had loved living in Korea with her grandmother and her parents. She had loved moving to Boston, where her mother went to college. She had loved moving to Los Angeles, where her mother went to medical school. When Lily's mother graduated, Lily was excited about moving to Chicago. That is, until Lily's parents told her they were here to stay.

"Ah," said Lily's father. "That's because there were Chinese immigrants coming here from many parts of China. Each group spoke different versions of the Chinese language."

Before they headed home, the family stopped at the Chicago Food Market. It was filled with bins of fresh fish. Chinese people were moving back and forth, looking for the freshest fish to buy. Lily's family bought some tasty fresh crabs.

Their last stop was Ping Tom Memorial Park. Lily saw a movie screen being set up. "They show movies here during the Summer Fun in Chinatown festival," Lily's dad said. "We'll come back another time."

On their way home on the rumbling "L," Lily couldn't stop smiling. "So," said her parents, "still want to move?"

Lily shook her head. "I have the whole world here in Chicago!" she said.

"Chicago has many different neighborhoods," Lily's mom told her. "You'll feel like you're living in many different places all at once."

Lily wasn't so sure. Staying in one place and one city seemed like the most boring thing in the world to her. Lily's mother had encouraged her to write everything down so she would remember it. So Lily took out the diary her grandmother had given her. It was called an *il gi,* and many Korean girls had one.

"Dear Diary," Lily wrote. "Please let us move soon."

Lily's dad had lived in Chicago years ago when he was in college. That made him feel like a native. "I want to show you around!" he said.

At C. W. Mei's Gift Shop, Lily's father picked up a *karate* outfit. Lily's grandmother bought some ginger tea at a tea and ginseng store. When Lily saw people doing the slow movements of *tai chi* on a street corner, she excitedly tried a few moves herself!

Everyone was speaking Chinese, but it didn't sound like the same Chinese language. Lily wanted to know why.

"I can tell from your expression, you want to keep exploring," said Lily's mother. Lily smiled. She knew how much fun it would be to take the "L" and walk to another Chicago neighborhood.

They got on the "L" and off they went. Lily's eyes opened wide. The streets were filled with *pagodas*, fish markets, and restaurants. All the signs were in Chinese. "We're in Chicago's Chinatown!" her father said.

Lily followed him outside. It was summer and very hot outside. "Remember how we always had to drive in Los Angeles?" he asked her. "Here, we can walk or take the local bus or train. That's much more fun, isn't it?"

"I guess," Lily said. She still wasn't sure how she felt about this new city.

They took the "L," or elevated train, to a neighborhood called Pilsen. Pilsen didn't look anything like Lily's neighborhood.

Everywhere Lily looked were colorful murals. Some of them had dancers painted on them. "This is the largest Mexican neighborhood in any city in the country," Lily's father told her. "Let's get an *enchilada* from this street vendor."

After they ate, they went to The Mexican Fine Arts Center Museum. "Did you know the first Mexicans came here in the early 1900s?" Lily's father asked her. "They worked in the steel mills."

"Hungry?" asked Lily's father. "Let's go to Bobak's Grocery Store."

Bobak's had one hundred different kinds of sausage! There were *kielbasa*, *kiszka*, and *bolszewik* hanging from the ceiling. "Let's try the gooseberry compote!" said Lily's mom.

"First it was like being in Mexico, and now it's like being in Poland," Lily said. "There are so many different neighborhoods."

Lily couldn't take her eyes off the paintings. There were large colorful paintings by Diego Rivera and Carmen Lomas Garza. There was also an exhibit of paintings of tiny little skeletons dressed up in all sorts of costumes. "Mexicans have a celebration called the Day of the Dead," said Lily's father. "They remember those who have died. They also celebrate the living."

"This neighborhood's big," said Lily. Her father nodded.

"The only bigger Polish neighborhood is Poland's capital city of Warsaw," he told her.

They walked past a church called St. Bruno's, on 48th Street. "This church holds services in the same way they have been done for centuries," Lily's father said. "Services are in Polish and English."

They wandered back onto the street. All the walking made Lily hungry. "I want an ice cream," Lily said.

"We're not going to get just any ice cream," Lily's father told her. "We're in a Mexican neighborhood. So we're getting Mexican ice cream!" Lily's father bought two Mexican *helados*...mango for himself and papaya for Lily. "*Gracias*," said Lily's father. That meant "thank you" in Spanish.

Lily and her dad passed kids playing in Harrison Park. They stopped at a grocery store. It was filled with all sorts of foods Lily had never seen before. Lily's dad picked up *chayote* cactus. "Maybe your mom can use this in some wonderful Mexican dish," he said.

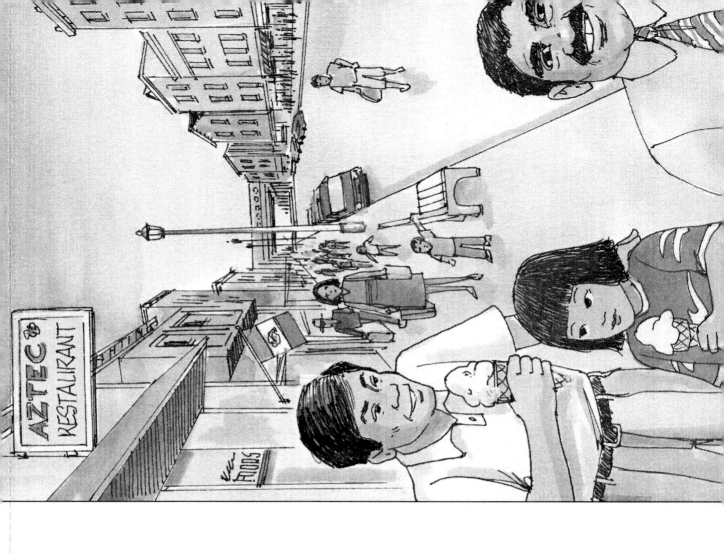

Just then, Lily heard some beautiful music. A young girl was playing a piano in the Polonia Book Store! "Piano lessons in a bookstore!" Lily said, amazed. The whole family stopped to listen.

"The study of music is important here," said Lily's father. "People support it just like in Korea." Lily could have stayed listening to the music forever, but her grandmother wanted to move on.

They walked past a beautiful old building. "It looks like an old theater," said Lily.

"It was," said her father. "Now it's the Copernicus Foundation Cultural and Civic Center. There are offices here and conference rooms to help support the Polish-American community."

"Did you have fun?" asked Lily's mother as Lily relaxed on the sofa at home.

"I did," she said. "It felt like we were in a city different from Chicago. I like feeling that I am not stuck in just one place."

"Well, then you will love our next visit," said Lily's dad. "I'm taking you, Grandma, and Mom to the Polish neighborhood!"

This time, when the family boarded the "L," Lily felt like an old pro.

"We're going to Archer Park," Lily's dad said. "Polish immigrants have been coming to settle in Chicago for many, many years. South Pulaski Avenue is the heart of their neighborhood. It's very social there."

© Pearson Education, Inc.

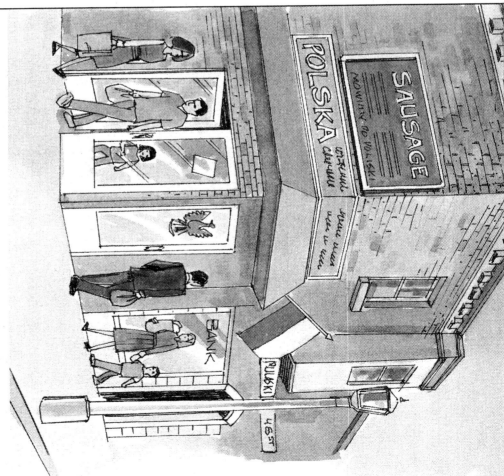

When they got off the "L," Lily pointed to a sign in the window of a bank. "What does that say?" she asked her father.

"*Mowimy po polsku* means 'we speak Polish,'" he said. "Many people here speak only Polish. These local businesses help the community by hiring people who speak Polish too."

Goldilocks and the Three Bears

by Rena Korb

Suggested levels for Guided Reading, DRA,™
Lexile,® and Reading Recovery™ are provided
in the Pearson Scott Foresman Leveling Guide.

Genre	Comprehension Skills and Strategy	
Animal fantasy	• Plot and Theme • Character • Visualize	

Scott Foresman Reading Street 3.6.4

ISBN 0-328-13407-4

PEARSON

Scott
Foresman

Vocabulary

crystal

disappeared

discovery

goal

journey

joyful

scoop

unaware

Word count: 1,102

Note: The total word count includes words in the running text and headings only. Numerals and words in chapter titles, captions, labels, diagrams, charts, graphs, sidebars, and extra features are not included.

Reader Response

1. Restate the events of the story. What happens in the beginning, the middle, and the end? What is the problem and solution that develop between the three bears and Goldilocks? Use a chart like this one to help put things in order.

Problem:
Beginning:
Middle:
End:
Solution:

2. When the Bear family returns from their trip, Billy Bear is joyful at the thought of eating his oatmeal. What words might describe Billy Bear in his kitchen?

3. Throughout the story, the Bear family and Goldilocks all make discoveries. List some of their discoveries.

4. What do you think about Billy Bear's and Goldilocks's actions? How would you have reacted if you were in their places?

Goldilocks and the Three Bears

by Rena Korb

illustrated by Sean O'Neill

Editorial Offices: Glenview, Illinois • Parsippany, New Jersey • New York, New York
Sales Offices: Needham, Massachusetts • Duluth, Georgia • Glenview, Illinois

Bears in the Wild

Wild bears live in North America, Europe, and Asia. Grizzly bears, black bears, and brown bears live in the United States. Bears live alone and rarely travel in groups.

Most bears will eat almost anything: fish, insects, other animals, seeds, roots, nuts, and berries. They also are very fond of ants and honey.

When bear cubs are born, they weigh only about a pound. The cubs stay with their mother for about a year and a half. She teaches them how to hunt, find food, and take care of themselves.

In the fall, bears eat a lot of food. Then they spend the next two to six months hibernating, or sleeping.

Later, Billy Bear and Goldilocks took a walk with Dad Bear to look for a tree trunk so Dad could make a new chair for Billy Bear.

At the end of the day, they all ate the special treats that Mom Bear had made: peanut butter and honey bars. Goldilocks said they were even more delicious than Billy Bear's oatmeal. "And my new friend is not too big or too small, or too anything! He's just right," she added.

Once upon a time, a family of bears lived in a green and leafy forest. These were no ordinary bears. Dad Bear was enormous. His bushy head almost brushed the top of the ceiling of their small house. Though much smaller than Dad, Mom Bear was still quite large. (She too was a bear, after all.)

Goldilocks stopped and turned around. She twisted her hair nervously between her fingers as she waited for Billy Bear to speak.

"Do you want to come and play with me?"

"Aren't you still mad that I ate your oatmeal and all that stuff?" Goldilocks asked.

"No," said Billy. "I forgive you."

"Wow, thanks, Billy! Let me just go ask my parents if it's okay."

"Hurry back," said Billy Bear.

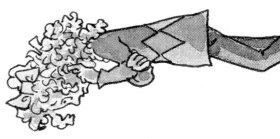

Dad and Mom Bear had a son named Billy Bear. Compared with his parents, Billy was a little bear. He was only in the third grade. He was also lonely. All of his classmates lived in the nearby town of Woodville and never came to see him after school.

Goldilocks looked at the three faces crowding around her. "I'm so-so-sorry," she stuttered. "I sm-smelled the yummy oat-oatmeal, so I climbed through the window and ate your breakfast. I'd better get on home now," she said. With a rush, she disappeared from the house.

"That little girl must be very lonely," said Dad Bear.

"Lonely?" repeated Billy. "She's just mean."

Mom said, "When people are lonely, they feel sad, but they act mean instead." Billy thought about that for a minute. He felt lonely too sometimes.

"Goldilocks!" Billy Bear called. "Wait a second!"

The bears' house was cheery and bright. At night, Dad Bear sat in his great big armchair. It was made out of a solid tree trunk that he and Billy had found in the forest. Mom Bear's smaller chair was covered in soft green velvet. Of course, Billy's chair was the smallest of all, but it fit him perfectly. Like Dad's chair, it was made of wood from the forest. Like Mom's chair, it was comfy with an embroidered cushion.

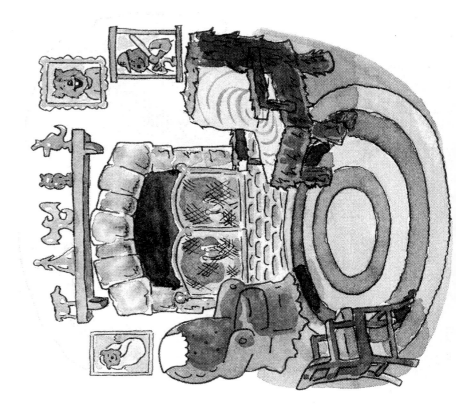

Upstairs were the bedrooms. Dad Bear had a great big bed with a thick mattress. Mom Bear had a medium-sized bed covered with a fleecy blanket. Billy Bear slept in a little bed carved out of cherry wood.

One morning, Mom decided to fix oatmeal for breakfast. She scooped it into bowls. Dad had a great big bowl, Mom had a medium-sized bowl, and Billy had a wee little bowl with just one scoop. When Billy tried to take a bite, he made a terrible discovery. The oatmeal was too hot to eat!

Dad Bear flung open Billy Bear's door. There Goldilocks slept like an angel. The intruder was just a little girl!

Billy Bear recognized Goldilocks by her long blond curls. "Goldilocks, you wake up right now!" he hollered, shaking her shoulders.

Goldilocks opened her eyes.

"What are you doing here?" Billy Bear demanded. "You ate my breakfast, you broke my chair, and now you're sleeping in my bed."

The Bear family decided to take a hike. Their goal was to let the oatmeal cool off. Now while they were on their journey, a little girl named Goldilocks wandered by their house.

Goldilocks was just about Billy Bear's age and even went to his school. Although she looked like a princess with her long golden curls, she sometimes acted as though everything in the world belonged to her.

Dad Bear went on a search of the house. "Stay behind me," he warned Mom Bear and Billy. They went into the family room.

"The intruder broke my crystal bunny!" complained Mom Bear.

"The intruder broke my chair!" wailed Billy Bear.

They checked the bedrooms next.

"Someone's been sleeping in both our beds," Mom Bear said.

"What's that delicious smell?" she wondered aloud. "It must be coming from this house." She peered through the window and saw that no one was at home. So, she climbed right into the bears' house!

First, she tasted Dad Bear's oatmeal. "Too hot!" Goldilocks cried. Next, she tried Mom Bear's oatmeal, but it was too cold. Then, she tried Billy Bear's oatmeal. It was so good that she licked the bowl clean.

"This must be Billy Bear's house!" she said, looking at photographs in the living room. Then she noticed Mom Bear's collection of delicate glass animals. She took a bunny off the shelf to get a closer look.

Then she sat in Dad Bear's big chair. "Oh, this is far too hard." Then she sat in Mom Bear's chair. "Oh, this is far too soft." Then she sat in Billy Bear's chair. "This is just right," she said. But suddenly, Billy Bear's chair collapsed beneath her, and the crystal bunny broke into tiny pieces.

Just then the Bear family returned home. Unaware that anyone had been in their house, Billy Bear ran to the kitchen, joyful at the thought of eating his oatmeal. Then they made the discovery.

"What's going on here?" Dad Bear said, racing in. They saw footprints across the floor, drips and drops of oatmeal on the kitchen table, and Billy Bear's bowl licked clean!

"Somebody's been eating my oatmeal," growled Dad Bear.

"Somebody's been eating my oatmeal," cried Mom Bear.

"Somebody's been eating my oatmeal and ate it all up," wailed Billy Bear.

They all turned to each other in shock. "Somebody's been in our house," the bears said.

Dad Bear stood tall and said with a roar, "I can take care of any intruders."

Goldilocks went upstairs and into Dad and Mom Bear's bedroom. She ran over to Dad Bear's bed, climbed up, and lay down to take a little nap. This bed was too hard.

Next, she tried Mom Bear's bed. She felt like she was trying to sleep on a marshmallow. It was simply too soft.

She struggled out of Mom Bear's bed and walked across the hallway. "This must be Billy Bear's room," she said.

Goldilocks saw Billy Bear's bed and lay down on it. It was just right! She stretched and yawned, and in a twinkling, Goldilocks was fast asleep.

Suggested levels for Guided Reading, DRA, Lexile,® and Reading Recovery™ are provided in the Pearson Scott Foresman Leveling Guide.

Social Studies

Genre	Comprehension Skills and Strategy	Text Features
Expository nonfiction	• Generalize • Author's Purpose • Predict	• Captions • Headings • Glossary • Map

Scott Foresman Reading Street 3.6.5

PEARSON
Scott Foresman

ISBN 0-328-13410-4
90000
9 780328 134106

Social Studies

Traditional Crafts of MEXICO

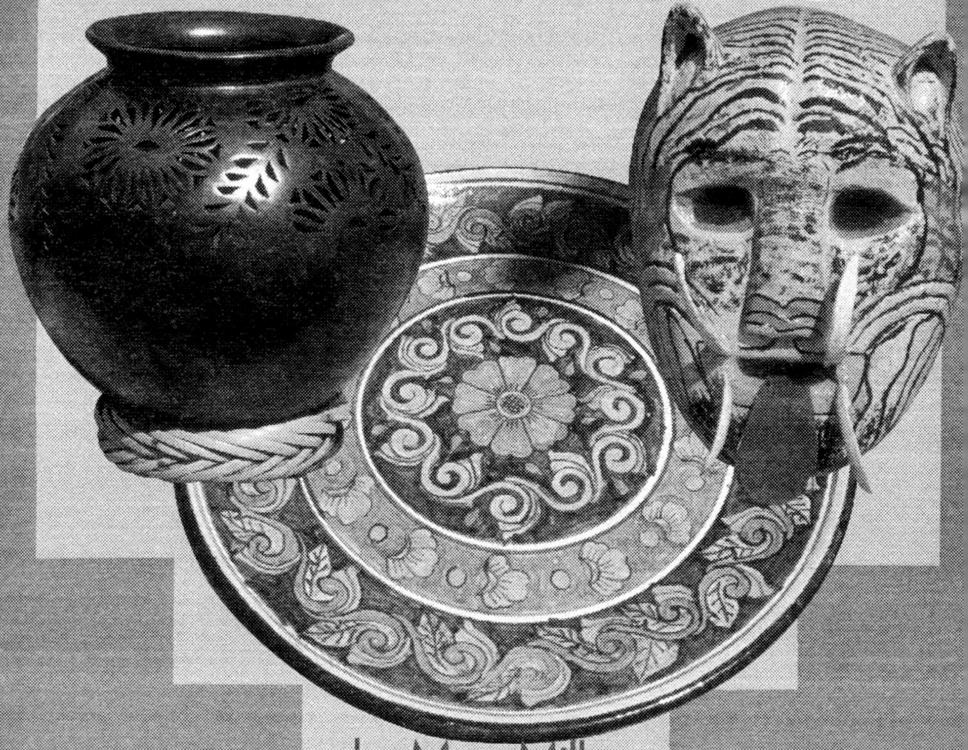

by Mary Miller

Vocabulary

burros

burst

factory

glassblower

puff

reply

tune

Word count: 1,053

Note: The total word count includes words in the running text and headings only.
Numerals and words in chapter titles, captions, labels, diagrams, charts, graphs,
sidebars, and extra features are not included.

Reader Response

1. What features do different Mexican crafts have in common? Use a simple web to show the features that are common to Mexican crafts.

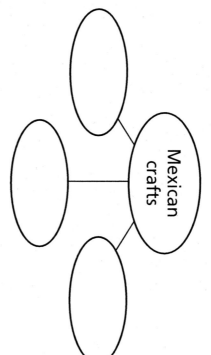

Mexican crafts

2. Predict what would happen to the traditional crafts of Mexico if people stopped teaching them to their children?

3. A compound word is a word made up of two smaller words. Find the compound word on the glossary list. From what two smaller words is it made? Use a dictionary to find other words using either of the smaller words.

4. Which of these traditional Mexican crafts would you most like to learn to make? Why?

Glossary

burros *n.* small donkeys

burst *v.* to break open suddenly

factory *n.* a building where things are made or built

glassblower *n.* a person who blows air into a heated lump of glass to make shapes

puff *v.* to blow in short breaths

reply *v.* to respond to an activity or answer a question

tune *n.* a piece of music; a melody

Traditional Crafts of Mexico

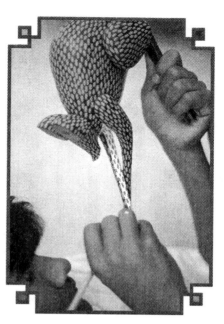

by Mary Miller

Editorial Offices: Glenview, Illinois • Parsippany, New Jersey • New York, New York
Sales Offices: Needham, Massachusetts • Duluth, Georgia • Glenview, Illinois

ISBN: 0-328-13410-4

A traditional papier-mâché skeleton

A Rich, Colorful History

Look around Mexico today, and you'll see colorful cloth, beautiful pottery, and brightly painted murals. These crafts go back thousands of years.

Mexico has a rich history of folk art. A folk artist is someone who makes a traditional craft. These crafts are made by hand in the artist's home. Most artists learn their crafts as children. They learn from family members. In this way, the craft is passed on from generation to generation.

The tradition of Mexican folk art has been passed on for thousands of years.

The Art of the Day of the Dead

Do you think skeletons are scary? Most Mexicans would **reply** that they are not. On November 2, people in Mexico celebrate *Dia de los Muertos*, or "Day of the Dead." Many Mexicans believe that death is not final. Rather, it is part of the cycle of life.

As with many events in Mexico, Dia de los Muertos has produced a tradition of craft forms. Artists make small, bright skeletons to sell. Many skeletons are made from papier-mâché. These happy skeletons are shown doing the activities people enjoy every day.

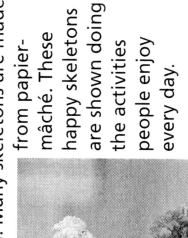

Flowers are placed on graves as part of the Dia de los Muertos celebration.

Ancient Indian Groups

Many Mexican crafts were first made by ancient Indian groups. They are still made the same way today. Some newer craft forms, such as glass blowing, were introduced by the Spanish. But a **glassblower** is rare in Mexico today, so the craft is dying out.

Before explorers from Spain discovered Mexico, powerful Indian groups ruled the land. These ancient peoples were the Maya and the Aztec. They were strong warriors. Their cities had great riches, with large amounts of gold. The Maya and the Aztec also created beautiful craft items.

The ruins of Tenochtitlan, an ancient city, are beneath modern Mexico City.

Needlework

Needlework is highly prized in Mexican culture. Many people wear shirts embroidered with bright colors and patterns. Most embroidery work is done by women. Girls learn needlework at a young age from their mothers and grandmothers. There are many beautiful embroidery designs.

People in Mexico wear their embroidery with pride.

17

The Maya

The Mayan civilization was at its peak from about A.D. 250 to A.D. 900. Mayan murals showed lifelike figures taking part in battles and festivals. The artists outlined the figures and then filled them in with color. A similar type of painting was used on Mayan pottery.

The Aztec

The Aztec ruled a mighty empire from 1400 to early 1500. Aztec craftspeople used feathers to make beautiful clothes and headdresses. Other important Aztec crafts were weaving, metalworking, pottery, and woodcarving.

Mayan artists decorated walls and buildings with brightly colored murals.

Wood Carving

During their rule, the Maya and Aztec peoples carved wood to make useful objects and decorations. Today, craftspeople carve wooden figures called *alebrijes*. These are Mexico's newest craft form. They were first made in small towns in Oaxaca fifty years ago. Often, these carvings show animals, fantastical creatures, or monsters. They are carved one at a time by hand, so no two carvings are ever the same.

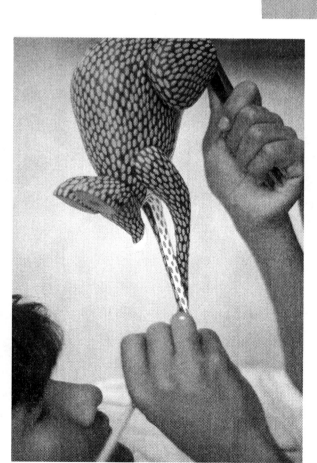

Once a carving is done, the figure is painted in bright colors.

Today, traditional Mexican crafts are made all over Mexico. You can find pottery in Mixteca, woven baskets in Veracruz, and masks in Oaxaca. You can find beautiful embroidered cloth in Acapulco. Every region has its own specialty.

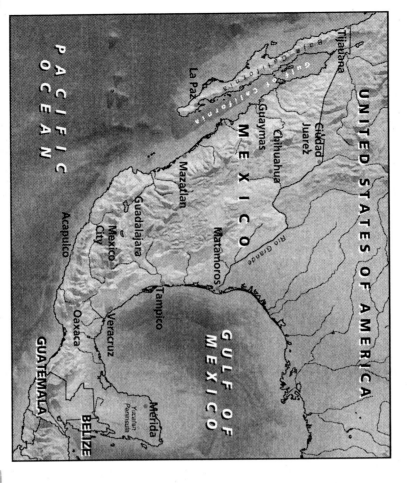

Mexicans still perform a dance called the *Tezcatlipoca*, or "smoking mirror." This dance is named for Tezcatlipoca, an invisible god who is shown as a black mirror. Tezcatlipoca's special animal was the jaguar. Dancers wear jaguar masks with mirrors set in the eyeholes.

Mexican people wear masks like this at traditional dances.

When the Spanish arrived, the native Indian groups learned new ways to make pottery.

One type of pottery is made only in Puebla, Mexico. This glazed, or shiny, pottery has been made the same way for nearly 500 years. Originally, blue was used on only the finest pieces because the color was very expensive. Other colors, such as green and yellow were introduced in the 1700s.

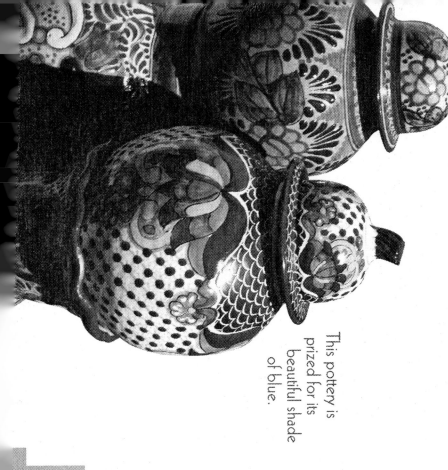

This pottery is prized for its beautiful shade of blue.

Oaxacan Black Pottery

Oaxacan potters use black clay to make their pottery. Special techniques are used to polish these pieces. The fine patterns on each piece are cut out by hand.

The region of Oaxaca is known for its black pottery.

11

After the pottery is fired, the bright colors are painted on by hand.

Weaving

Indians were weaving in the valleys of Oaxaca as long ago as 500 B.C. After they were taken over by the Aztec, their woven clothes became valuable.

Today, Oaxacan weavers still create beautiful wool rugs. Each rug is woven by hand on a loom. Many weavers use natural dyes. The colors come from animals, plants, and minerals. These dyes produce beautiful colors that do not fade or rub off.

An artist can work for 300 hours to create one rug.

Mexican Pottery

Pottery is one of the oldest crafts in Mexico. Most Mexican pottery is made by hand. The clay pieces are shaped and then dried. The dried pieces are then painted with geometric patterns.

In the countryside, ancient ways of making pottery are still used today. For example, Mixteca Indian women still dig clay from the earth. They use this clay to make bowls, cups, and dishes. Sometimes they make vases, statues, or flutes to **puff** into and play a simple **tune**. After the clay pieces dry out in the air, they are fired in an open pit. Until they are fired, they must be handled carefully so they do not **burst**.

Traditional Mexican potters shape clay by hand.

Basket Weaving

Weaving beautiful and useful things from reeds and palm leaves is one of Mexico's oldest crafts. Weavers use Mexican bamboo and palm leaves to make baskets, hats, and mats.

The weavers use natural dyes to color the reeds and leaves in deep shades of blue, red, and purple. The dyed reeds are then woven by hand into beautiful patterns. In some Veracruz towns, women can weave as many as twenty baskets a day.

Weaving has changed very little over thousands of years.

Modern Mexican Crafts

In the 20th century, many poor people left the countryside to find **factory** jobs in the city. Some traveled on foot, and others came on **burros.**

But not all things made in Mexico today come from factories. In the villages, Mexican folk artists still make crafts. They work in the same way as the ancient peoples of Mexico.

Folk artists take their crafts to the village market to sell to tourists.

Masks

People in Mexico have been making masks for thousands of years. The first known mask was made about 12,000 B.C. The mask looked like a coyote's head. Many masks were made of gold and precious stones, such as turquoise and coral.

The Spanish introduced the custom of wearing masks at dances. Today, masks are worn in Mexico during festivals and celebrations. Some masks look like animals. Some masks are carved from wood and painted in bright colors. Other masks are made from colorful beads. Often, masks are decorated with colorful feathers for hair.

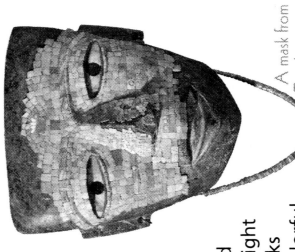

A mask from Teotihuacán